Sanctuary

of

Healing

Sanctuary
of
Healing

TRANSFORMING CHURCHES
INTO TRAUMA-INFORMED SPACES

Julia Matallana Freedman

Church
PUBLISHING

Church Publishing
19 East 34th Street
New York, NY 10016
www.churchpublishing.org

Cover design by Newgen
Typeset by Nord Compo

ISBN 978-1-64065-821-9 (paperback)
ISBN 978-1-64065-822-6 (eBook)

Library of Congress Control Number: 2025934503

Para mi familia.

To my daughter, my brightest *estrella*. May you always know that you carry generations of love, strength, and resilience in your body. You are the future of our *familia*, the living proof that our stories endure. May you walk boldly, speak your truth, and never doubt how fiercely you are loved.

To my husband, Jesse, my companion, my cheerleader, and my rock. Your unwavering belief in me has been my refuge and my fire. You remind me that love is not just something we inherit—it is something we build, fiercely and faithfully, every single day.

Familia is more than blood; it is the unbreakable thread that ties past, present, and future together. This is for us all.

Contents

Foreword

*I*n recent decades, the Christian community has begun a profound reckoning with the realities of trauma, moving beyond the simple binaries of sin and redemption to embrace a more complex understanding of human suffering. This transformation is part of a broader cultural shift that acknowledges the deep wounds many carry, wounds that do not fit neatly into the traditional categories of pastoral care. In this context, *Sanctuary of Healing* stands as a critical contribution, challenging the Church to become a more responsive, empathetic, and healing community.

Rev. Julia's work is both deeply personal and theologically robust, drawing on her lived experiences as a pastor, her multicultural heritage, and her journey as a survivor of trauma. This is not a detached manual of theory; it is a work born from the trenches of real ministry, where pain and grace often walk side by side. Her reflections on the complexities of trauma resonate with the raw honesty of someone who has not only walked this path but has also chosen to guide others along it.

In these pages, Rev. Julia tackles the intricate dance between faith and trauma, insisting that Christian theology must grapple with the embodied, messy, and often nonlinear nature of healing. Her reflections echo the wisdom of theologians like Serene Jones and Shelley Rambo, who have argued for a more embodied, less triumphalist understanding of resurrection and redemption. Rev. Julia invites us to see scars not as symbols of weakness, but as signs of survival and strength, drawing upon the deep wells of biblical imagery, from the wounded Christ to the grieving Psalms.

What sets this work apart is its insistence on community as the context for healing. Freedman rightly contends that trauma is not merely a private wound but a communal concern. In a world fractured by racial violence, political unrest, climate change, and the enduring legacies of colonization, this book calls the Church to be a place of radical, collective care—a sanctuary in the truest sense. At a time when so many are searching for spiritual homes where they can bring their whole selves, trauma and all, *Sanctuary of Healing* offers a vital road map. It is a call to the Church to rediscover its vocation as a place of refuge, not just for the soul, but for the whole person, embodying the incarnational love of Christ in all its gritty reality.

This book is an invitation to pastors, lay leaders, and parishioners alike to move beyond the platitudes that too often characterize religious responses to suffering and to embrace the complex, sacred work of healing. It is a courageous, timely, and necessary offering for a Church in desperate need of renewal. I commend this work to you, trusting that it will inspire a new generation of healers, community builders, and cycle-breakers. May we have the courage to build the sanctuaries of healing that our fractured world so urgently needs.

Prof. John Swinton
University of Aberdeen, Scotland
May 2025

A Sacred Story: Why This Book Matters

> The Latino story is about survival, it's about how we've managed to keep our sense of dignity and humanity through years of colonization, displacement, and struggle. Our stories are sacred because they're proof that we are still here, still dreaming, still healing.
>
> —Sandra Cisneros,
> Chicana writer and author of
> *The House on Mango Street*

Reading This Book as a Journey

One of my biggest fears about ministry is that I'm too wounded to be a "professional Christian." But I've come to realize that this is the wrong way to think about my own personal trauma. Ultimately, pain and resilience mingle together, side by side. We mustn't ignore one or the other.

I was adopted into a Colombian family as an infant, but biologically I am Singaporean. I didn't discover this until later in life, and as a result, my sense of identity is layered and evolving. Suffice it to say, I grew up believing I was of Colombian ancestry, and I am very proud of my Colombian family and all that I was socialized to become during the entirety of my childhood and young adult years.

My Colombian grandfather flew to Austria to hear me play viola during college. No one in our family had ever completed a four-year university, and I felt the weight of carrying their hopes and dreams on my shoulders. My dad's family had come to America seeking a better life, and this—me traveling abroad with my college orchestra, performing the Brandenburg Viola Concerto in small Hungarian and Austrian churches—was one way they saw that dream becoming real. It was a magnificent honor. Naturally, my family—adopted or not—wouldn't miss the chance to celebrate that milestone with me.

Amid these rich experiences of love and support, questions about belonging—and about the idea of Father, both earthly and divine—have lingered. That's a story for another book. For now, what's most important is that I was raised in a mixed-race family as the eldest daughter of a Colombian immigrant. That's where my family name, Matallana, comes from—having originated in Spain (yes, likely colonizers).

I haven't fully unraveled what it means to be functionally "tri-ethnic," but for the sake of this work, I speak from the perspective of someone who grew up in a Colombian-American family.

In the pages that follow, I write about some of my own trauma. When I'm writing about others some names and details have been adjusted to protect privacy or emphasize certain aspects of trauma. It is my hope that my own story of nonlinear healing will offer support, friendship, and maybe even a companion on your own journey. It's a pastoral book, as well as a practical book.

Faith and Wounds: Embracing Both

I want to make abundantly clear that this work would not have been possible without the very Christian communities that have been around me at almost every point of my life. And while I identify as a progressive Christian, even my experience in less progressive parish settings have offered me some of the greatest Christian hope I could have needed in that moment. They offered me community, unconditional love, and in some cases, a free place to live or spend the night when I wasn't able to find a safe place. It is the best and brightest parts of the Christian community that have helped me heal my soul, and I don't think that is anything but deeply spiritual. I have been immensely blessed that over the last decade and a half, each parish I have served in has taught me something incredibly important about who God is, about what Christian community can look like. Every story shared is meant to express my gratitude and awe of God at work in our world, and I trust that you, dear reader, will see these stories as such.

To offer a bit more context even still, it was within my part-Colombian immigrant family that the stories passed down were of a very specific variety. I suppose they were stories of trauma, but I never really thought of them in that way. In our mostly white suburban neighborhood, in our cookie-cutter home where a plush carpet lay soft beneath our feet, my dad would tell me and my sisters his stories.

These stories were about his home with a dirt floor in rural Colombia. They were about how he had never seen canned vegetables until he arrived in the States. That he and his sisters would pile up on a single banana-seat bicycle, with a three-legged boxer dog cruising next to them. He and his sisters would take care of injured birds.

I can almost picture this simple, family-centered life, a life nestled between the two main mountain ranges in Colombia. The thick lush leaves drenched in morning dew and magical realism. I can imagine my dad killing the chickens in the backyard for dinner and helping defeather them so his family could all eat together. But these stories were never told as "trauma." These stories of poverty, and even the stories of war, were just . . . life.

When I was young my stories were often met with "*Sana sana colita de rana . . .*,"[1] which was mostly used for a physical ailment of some kind. But the same mentality existed around

---

1   Translated to: "heal, heal, little frog's tail." This is a common children's rhyme used when a child gets hurt, particularly in Latin American and Spanish-speaking cultures.

emotional trauma too. Like so many non-Black people of color, my family valued assimilation. I remember feeling embarrassed when friends asked where my dad was from because of his accent. When I'd say he was Colombian, it was often followed by some stereotypical "joke" about him having access to cocaine—just because of Colombia's historic association with it. In reality, my dad had absolutely no connection to that world. Even as a kid, I never found those comments funny.

My white mother didn't have the resources to help me understand my racial identity. Instead, she would talk about the American Dream, Manifest Destiny, American greatness. In her view, I could do anything because this was America. Even though I have a complex relationship with this belief, I wonder if it has somehow sustained my willingness to simply put myself and my work out into the world and hope that someone will resonate with it.

I'm a committed cycle breaker. When I was just fifteen years old, I made a commitment to myself to do everything I could in my life to break cycles of abuse and oppression within my family systems. Unlike previous generations within my family of origin, I don't want to stick my head in the sand. I'm not interested in hiding our stories of struggle and despair. I have found that ignoring one's pain can inadvertently cause harm to others and runs the likely risk of perpetuating the same cycles of abuse, colonization, and harm.

Eventually, the urge to undo harm bled into my ministry life. I realized that I wanted to see cycles of racism, misogyny, colonialism, and spiritual and religious abuse end within the Christian church. I do not claim to know how to do this perfectly, or even at all. Nor do I have an answer about how to decolonize our tradition. But just like my commitment to myself in 2006, as a fifteen-year-old suffering from daily traumas, I see a better path forward. A path of contagious resilience, a path of healing rituals, and a life of meaning and purpose.

Part of being in beloved community with one another means being open to the ways that trauma impacts our current lives. I don't want to ignore the impact of trauma in our religious communities anymore.

I must confess, I'm an idealist. Perhaps that will be intensely obvious throughout this book, but part of my personal resilience in the face of very serious trauma means that I see the possibility for restoration and healing wherever I look. I believe, even in an institution that has historically caused a great deal of harm, that there can be genuine healing as a Christian community. We can be cycle breakers! You can be a cycle breaker too!

We, as a Christian community, must safely, delicately, and with wisdom and grace, offer spaces of emotional and spiritual healing. I believe we can offer greater hope and purpose in one's life. And we can offer, discuss, and experiment with a variety of spiritual practices and rituals that parishioners may find healing. It's an individual enterprise but it is also deeply communal too.

And I'm not talking about the kind of healing that one might see in, say, a Pentecostal church. The kind of miraculous healing that happens from one moment to the next. I don't believe trauma is healed that way. Trauma is always a struggle. And struggle is not a bad thing. In all truth, it can even be a good thing, an important part of the healing process.

Struggle means you've delved deep into the trauma and wrestled with the stories you've told yourself and the lies you may have come to believe about God, about yourself, or about humanity. I've had to struggle for the peace that I have now. Sometimes with trauma it feels like things get a little worse before they get better. I'm not going to sugarcoat anything. You may have to give yourself some extended time, space, and better care. You may need to prioritize your mental well-being in this season. It's okay. Take your time and don't rush through this work. It's supposed to be hard-won. It's also well worth it. And I'm right here with you.

This book relies on the social sciences and the field of psychology to understand how certain religious practices can actually heal these deep wounds. But that doesn't mean the pain isn't still there. Trauma demands that something of the wound remains no matter where you are in your healing journey. Like much of our Christian life, this, too, is a lifelong venture. Scarring is the best analogy of how this works.

Wounded people can offer hope to others when the wounds have healed and become scars. Henri Nouwen would agree. Jesus was raised from the dead and the scars remained; in fact, some of his disciples even demanded to see those scars. Scars are intensely important to the Easter narrative! They don't disappear. And to demand to see the remnants of one another's scars is deeply human.

One of the most critical components of a trauma-informed space is recognizing our own limitations in this field. Whether you are a lay leader or a professional clergy-person, our limitations must remain centrally critical. While I fully believe Christ can heal, we are not Christ, God's Holy Spirit, or clinical physicians.

Faith and Mental Health: There Is No Conflict

Early in my career as a pastor, a dear friend of mine, who knew I was attending seminary, would regularly text me to ask about her mental-health medications. One of the truisms I stated, and restated, was that I'm not a physician, and she should feel empowered to speak with those professionals in her life. However, I did share how God has given humanity all realms of healing practices to undergird our lives. God has given us psychiatrists, therapists, psychologists, as well as Eastern medicine to help those who have experienced trauma. These professionals will be a guiding force in the chapters ahead.

My friend's query about medication and her prayer life illustrated a real conundrum for some people. Her central question—"Am I not praying enough if I have to take these medications?"—made it clear that she was wondering if she was a bad Christian because she had to take a medication. This stigma still exists in some spaces and for some individuals. Therefore, I want to emphasize at the outset that there is no competition between these clinical professionals and one's prayer life. They can work hand in hand, as God has given us these clinical professions to help heal our souls.

Naming these important limitations for clergypeople and lay leaders is vital. I spoke with another young person who had an experience with a clergyperson who authentically walked with them into psychological hospitalization. When the parishioner made their suicidal thoughts known to this clergyperson, the latter was able to offer companionship and a referral that may have saved the parishioner's life. She told the parishioner to pack a bag and that she would pick them up and drive them to an evaluator. She explained the process of being evaluated and admitted into a psychiatric setting, offering a road map of expectations for the parishioner to ease the transition. She offered support to get them the help they needed.

This example illustrates how the clergyperson immediately recognized the need for a referral. And not only that, in the parishioner's moment of need, she offered to

xxii   Sanctuary of Healing

accompany them to the facility that was recommended. By
the very nature of it, mental-health hospitalization can be
inherently traumatic. Even the physical reality of going to a
hospital can be traumatic. One must leave one's friends and
family, as many did during COVID-19, a time when many
hospitals didn't allow visitors due to important public health
requirements. This can be an event that feels like your life is
slipping away from you.

However, as in the case above, the clergyperson had built
up enough rapport with the parishioner that they trusted her
to accompany them into this initial and important step of
hospitalization. Furthermore, this clergyperson visited them
in the hospital and wrote notes of encouragement regularly.

One tricky piece about trauma is that it doesn't stay in
the past. One's trauma leaks into the present and sometimes
it overtakes the present.[2] Normalizing the reality of how
trauma impacts humans can open up conversation, create a
safe space, foster deeper belonging, and allow individuals to
face their own trauma with bravery. A *supportive community*
coupled with a *culture of validation* makes for a powerful
recipe toward being more trauma-informed.

But how do we get there? This book shares how and
why a religious community can begin to be shaped into an
eclectic, trauma-informed one. What you will notice is that

---

2   Another clinical term for this might be "flashbacks" or "emotional flashbacks."
Pete Walker explains this in depth. Walker, *Complex PTSD*, 3.

all of my suggestions are founded on the principle that this work of healing trauma is best done in community. It's an activity that must be rooted in relationships with other people because no one should have to bear their suffering alone.

Trauma isn't something that happened in the past and therefore should stay in the past. *No!* It pervades our present, and in the case of generational trauma, it pervades the future, too. Dr. Shelley Rambo, a professor of theology from Boston University who specializes in the intersection of trauma and theology, puts it this way: "The past does not stay, so to speak, in the past. Instead, it invades the present, returning in such a way that the present becomes not only an enactment of the past but an enactment about what was not fully known or grasped."[3] When the trauma of our past invades the present, it impacts the entire community. If one parishioner in the community relives a traumatic sexual experience with her stepfather every time the Lord's Prayer is read because of the use of the word "father," that impacts the entire community—not just the one who bears the wounds. Or I believe, at the least, it should. I will develop this more later on. If we believe in the power of the Christian community—if we believe in the incarnational Christ who gives us an example of the way of love—one wound such as this should impact the community as a whole. It should shape the decisions we make in our worship, it should be

---

3   Rambo, *Spirit and Trauma*, 19.

part of the conversation for that community if those wounds do indeed exist.

Therefore, healing is really twofold. A supportive community with a culture of validation *plus* a community that recognizes how trauma does not stay precisely in the past are both needed to invigorate our parishes toward being more trauma-informed. This book is going to offer you suggestions and examples of both.

Healing Is a Community Effort

I'd encourage you to gather your community to discuss the contents of this book because this is work that must be done with many perspectives in mind. It must be balanced and multidimensional, as new research in trauma studies comes out, and always human-centered. Dr. Rev. Serene Jones, the president of Union Theological Seminary and a theology and trauma scholar, says that "traumatic events are over-whelming" insofar as they are experienced as inescapable and unmanageable. They outstrip our capacity to respond to and cope with them. Like the wave of a tsunami, they drown you and disable your normal strategies for dealing with difficulties. You lose a sense of yourself as someone who can take effective action against an attacking agent because, at a literal level, either you cannot fight back, or if you do, you fail. These events also overwhelm your capacity to make intelligible sense of them because they are stronger and more intense than the best meaning-making strategy you have. In this regard, they override your powers of both action and imagination."[4] Dr. Rev. Serene Jones clearly reminds us that when your senses are overloaded and you lack the ability to respond or even evaluate a situation, this is why the work of healing must be done within the community. We need each other.

---

4   *Trauma and Grace: Theology in a Ruptured World*. By Serene Jones. Louisville, Ky.: Westminster John Knox Press, 2009. 200 pp.

Introduction

> There has to be something in you, something
> that hungers for clarity. And you will need that
> hunger, because if you follow that path, soon
> enough you will find yourself confronting
> not just their myths, not just their stories, but
> your own.
>
> —Ta-Nehisi Coates[1]

During my second year of college at Westmont College in the hills of Montecito, in Santa Barbara County, California, the picturesque setting, resembling the rolling hills of an Italian winery, was devastatingly disrupted. The Tea Fire of 2008 burned hundreds of homes, and the fire spread rapidly due to the warm California winds—the Sundowner and Santa Ana winds. Many students evacuated immediately, but as an underclassman without a car, I was sent to our gymnasium, the firesafe zone. I grabbed

---

1 Ta-Nehisi Coates, *The Message*, 19.

the two most important possessions I had: my viola and my Bible. Hundreds of students spent the night in the gym, filled with smoke but well monitored and protected by our great firefighters of Santa Barbara County.

The aftermath for Westmont College and its faculty housing was significant. While there were no fatalities, the physics lab, psychology building, math building, and fifteen of the faculty homes were destroyed. Two of the buildings in Clark Residence Hall were completely gutted, along with the resident director's cottage. The effects were wide-reaching. This was my first experience where a Christian institution offered therapy and trauma resources after a devastating natural disaster.

Getting back to class took weeks. Many areas of campus remained closed for extended periods, and exams were ultimately canceled. The aftereffects of this trauma took time to heal, even though wildfires are now commonplace each summer and fall in California. Getting back to life as usual, rebuilding, and restoring can overshadow the ongoing effects of such a disaster.

Trauma is not new.

This book seeks to touch on several forms of trauma and how church communities might play a healing role in the lives of their parishioners. This book is designed for clergy, lay leaders, and anyone who wants to see our churches be places of belonging and healing, instead of shame and control.

As a clergyperson, some of the forms of trauma that I have seen impact the communities I've served include:

- racial trauma
- domestic violence
- religious trauma
- grief
- mental health trauma
- political trauma
- trauma caused by climate change
- adverse childhood experiences
- the global pandemic (which included traumas around wealth disparities, race, and health)

I will address each in the chapters ahead.

Much of the earliest studies on trauma were around military men and women returning from combat, and it is important to understand that the field developed within this context. Shelley Rambo says, "The cycles of war in the twentieth century have taken posttraumatic stress disorder (PTSD) out of the private sphere and identified it as a political and national diagnosis."[2] Similarly, Bessel van der Kolk's premier work, *The Body Keeps the Score*, begins with the groundbreaking work he was doing with veterans. He says, "A turning point arrived in 1980, when a group of

---

2   Rambo, *Spirit and Trauma*, 3.

Vietnam veterans, aided by the New York psychoanalysts Chaim Shatan and Robert J. Lifton, successfully lobbied the American Psychiatric Association to create a new diagnosis: posttraumatic stress disorder (PTSD). . . . With the conceptual framework of PTSD in place, the stage was set for a radical change in our understanding of our patients. This eventually led to an explosion of research and attempts at finding effective treatments."[3]

The field of trauma studies has deepened and widened dramatically since then. Today, PTSD is a diagnosis used for so much more than just veterans who experienced combat. For example, Generation Z is now known as the "most anxious generation,"[4] and PTSD may not be far from an answer as to why. Gen Zers all grew up with active-shooter drills, some even experiencing shootings. Many lived through—from a young age—both 9/11 and the global pandemic, two major, corporate, and societal traumas. Remarkably, Generation Z is the most open to talking about mental-health concerns and voicing their felt anxiety. Trauma is now a mainstream topic, and conversations on the topic of trauma are readily accessible through popular articles, social media, and free podcast content.

But even without a PTSD diagnosis, trauma can impact many areas of life. The CDC states that 64 percent of adults in

---

3   van Der Kolk, *The Body Keeps the Score*, 19.
4   "How Worried Should People Be About Generation Z?" *Economist*, March 15, 2024, https://www.economist.com/culture/2024/03/15/how-worried-should-people-be-about-generation-z.

the United States have experienced at least one adverse child-hood experience.[5] They also state that "one in 4 women and about one in 26 men have experienced completed or attempted rape. About one in nine men were made to penetrate someone during his lifetime. One in three women and about one in nine men experienced sexual harassment in a public place."[6] These statistics impact our parishioners and give us a window into the variety of trauma that folks carry within our ministry contexts.

In this book, you will discover why giving voice to the stories that define us, particularly the traumatic stories, is so critical to the enterprise of healing from trauma. A wide-reaching case in point is found in the #MeToo movement. Many of us recall the extensive social influence that some women may have collectively felt while sharing their stories of sexual trauma. Realizing you are not alone is a critical piece of the process of healing, and listening to one another brings about strength, community, and genuine healing.

At this inflection point, the church has an opportunity to become a healing space for individuals to recover and rebuild. Amid very real trauma, we can ask questions about our humanity and what it means to be a follower of Christ. It is in Christ's healing that the Church can begin to find its way again in all the uncertainty facing our communities.

---

5   "Adverse Childhood Experiences," Centers for Disease Control, accessed March 25, 2025, https://www.cdc.gov/violenceprevention/aces/index.html.
6   "Sexual Violence Prevention," Centers for Disease Control, accessed March 25, 2025, https://www.cdc.gov/sexual-violence/about/.

People are looking for healing spaces in their lives. They are searching for community and in-person places to meet, gather, and worship, bringing all that truly matters with them. They are looking for spiritual depth that speaks to the trauma, violence, war, and suffering in our broken world. Gone are the days of Sunday morning platitudes—the urgency of addressing the very real trauma in our world is a matter of life and death.

What I mean by life and death is that trauma, in any form, can *feel* like life and death. Overwhelming anxiety can feel like life and death. Mental illness can be (and also feel like) life and death. LGBTQ+ discrimination can mean (and feel like) life and death, particularly if we understand that life means living into one's unique identity, bringing all that they are to their in-person relationships. In her book *Trauma and Grace*, Dr. Rev. Serene Jones says: "A traumatic event is one in which a person or persons perceives themselves or others as threatened by an external force that seeks to annihilate them and against which they are unable to resist and which overwhelms their capacity to cope."[7]

With this definition in mind, the significant question of this book is, "How can we create spaces of healing for those with traumatic experiences in our religious spaces?" I contend that it is imperative to the future of the church that our religious spaces be more trauma-informed. While clergy

---

7   Serene Jones, *Trauma and Grace*, 29.

have limitations in this field, which I will delve into more deeply in the following chapters, we have a chance to ask the question for our parishioners, "How does trauma impact our humanity?"

Trauma can be an equalizer because it acknowledges that the world is broken, and we are all part of that very broken world. It is not lost on me that religion has historically been a culprit of so much harm and trauma. The pages that follow are an excellent primer on how to become a more trauma-informed community.

Sanctuary of Healing grapples with important questions such as:

- How do clergy grapple with their own trauma in a healthy way?
- How do clergy and church leaders create space for deeper community and stronger interpersonal support?
- What resources exist to help support one's efforts?
- What is the basic biology behind the trauma response?
- What are some examples of intergenerational and racial trauma?
- How does the liminal space between Good Friday and Easter Sunday offer hope for the traumatized?

This enterprise is inherently ecclesiological. It's about creating a particular culture within a group of people—God's people—a culture of emotional and psychological safety, a culture of anti-bullies and peacemakers.

In the pages that follow, I bare my soul and offer practical tools and further reading to deepen the Church's reach in order to foster God's healing touch in the lives of every person we encounter. At the end of this book, I offer an in-depth primer on domestic violence, racial trauma, and spiritual/religious trauma, including a broad definition, a prayer that can be used in parish settings when appropriate, and further resources. I try to grapple with how trauma intersects with issues like systemic injustice, racial inequity, and economic disparity. This primer is a simple tool to start the conversation within your context and begin to foster a more trauma-informed religious community.

In this work, I endeavor to never assume someone *hasn't* experienced what I speak about. Or put more simply, I always assume someone has a personal experience based on the type of trauma I am speaking about. This outlook has helped me prepare words that are trauma-informed. For example, even though I do not have a personal experience with gun violence, I assume when talking on the subject that someone in my presence just might have that raw personal experience. This allows me to approach the topic with sensitivity and care. Likewise, I have tried my best to write in a sensitive and pastoral manner. My hope is that you may be challenged by this book, but not retraumatized by it. The examples I have chosen, I believe, are gentle, on purpose.

In part, what the Church has to offer is a mending of the mind-body relationship around the experience of trauma. It is through our embodied religious practices that we can tap into the hope and life that Christ offers all of us in healing.

I want to begin this effort with two religious practices that offer me immense hope in my own healing, and I trust that they offer something important for your work as well. As mentioned before, embodied prayer practices can begin to mend the mind-body relationship after a traumatic experience. Your body is a wonder, no matter what your ability, or physical condition. Your mind and body were made to inform each other, and that relationship between your mind and body is an important one and a relationship that deserves your attention, care, and consideration. The mind-body connection deeply informs my pastoral work.

The physical embodiment of our prayer practices will continue to be a guiding principle to creating trauma-informed spaces. I want to begin this work with two mind-body forms of prayer. Consider each, and perhaps try one or both for an extended period of time. This work takes time, and you should allow yourself to embark at a pace that is suitable for you. I share these practices as a gift to your very heart and spirit. To remind you that your pain matters, your suffering matters, and your trauma matters, especially to God. A God who loves all of you, all of who you are, and doesn't look at trauma as something that has tainted a good thing. Trauma is part of the human condition. And God sees it fully and loves us regardless.

Centering Prayer

Centering prayer is a form of meditation. Meditation. Yes, I know, I sound like a hippy-dippy Southern Californian. That may be true, but much of my own personal trauma work has deepened and *depended* on my relationship with meditation. I meditate nearly every day! I use apps, and I have excerpts from The Book of Common Prayer in prominent places in my home around activities and challenges I face.

For example, the prayer in the "Ministration to the Sick" for the lack of sleep is a very powerful prayer that I use often when my sleep is disrupted. It's not a quick fix, and sometimes I still don't sleep, but just having these Christian words nearby gives me comfort.

While the word "meditation" may mean many things, let me share my understanding. Meditation is first and foremost a form of prayer. But it's also a way of controlling the mind. It requires being present within the body as you engage with the control of your thoughts. Meditation, including deep breathing, bodily relaxation, and a settled mind, helps to activate the parasympathetic nervous system. The very system that can help regulate our responses and emotions.

When I hold space for centering prayer or meditation, I move my body into a restful position, often cross-legged on the floor or seated in a chair with my feet flat on the floor. I try to remember how the floor space I occupy touches the earth, and the earth connects us all. This phrase grounds me. It's not transcendental for me; rather, it is bodily. It also reminds me that I'm just one human being, and the smallness and the human connection between me and those I love is comforting.

When my mind drifts, and it does often, I don't get caught up in the shame or a cycle of self-criticism. I see distraction as part of the human experience. I try to acknowledge the thought or worry and let it float away, like clouds. You don't feel shame when a cloud floats by you, and this should help you realize that your thoughts are nothing more than thoughts. They aren't reality, they don't define you and you can let them float by.

If you wanted to attempt this exercise, I would encourage you to imagine your worries as clouds and let them float away. Or perhaps imagine them as bubbles that can pop and disappear. Find an image that is fragile and temporary and that works for you. Additionally, I often set up a "healing sounds" playlist to help focus my time.

Tip:

You can search for "healing sounds" on most services where you can listen to music. I happen to use a playlist I made on Spotify. When you search "healing sounds," many recordings of Eastern singing bowls pop up. You may even be able to find something soothing to listen to on YouTube or Pandora.

Sometimes I use a phrase or word as a mantra to focus on during my 10–15 minutes of centering prayer or meditation. You might start by asking God for that word or phrase. If God offers something clear, hang onto that phrase or word for this extended period of time. If God does not offer a word of phrase, that's OK. Perhaps you can use a phrase you have memorized already, a piece of scripture or a portion of the Lord's Prayer. Try to let your imagination play with the phrase or word. You could invite God to help you understand why this word or phrase might be important at this time.

Finally, it is important to gradually move from meditation back to consciousness. I start by wiggling my toes and fingers, bringing life, slowly, back into my body. I open my eyes and look at the room around me as I come back, in order to become fully present within my own body.

I have much more to share about journaling, but I'd encourage you to write about your experience with this. You may discover even more if you give yourself some time to process what you have experienced. It's okay to be honest if this didn't work for you. You can write about that frustration, and your experience may lead to a different kind of breakthrough. And remember: Like any skill, meditation takes a lot of practice. I have found that some of those anxious pastoral thoughts begin to shrink down once you practice this regularly. You may even bounce back quicker from the ups and downs of pastoral ministry.

Anglican Prayer Beads

Anglican prayer beads are a beautiful and historic spiritual practice. Their origins trace back to second-century Hinduism, where they were used for counting prayers. Similarly, some Catholics use the rosary as a form of prayer beads.

For me, the significance of prayer beads lies in their embodied nature. Holding them, counting each bead, and feeling their smooth texture between my fingers engages both the mind and body. This tactile practice fosters a sense of calm, grounding, and presence.

The Anatomy of Anglican Prayer Beads

Anglican prayer beads consist of:

1. An invitatory bead to begin.
2. Four cruciform beads, dividing the circle into four sections.
3. Twenty-eight smaller beads, known as the "weeks."

Jennifer Gamber provides a thoughtful approach to incorporating Anglican prayer beads into personal devotion. She suggests choosing four simple prayers, which could come from The Book of Common Prayer or other sources.[8] One method she recommends includes:

---

8 *My Faith, My Life: A Teen's Guide to the Episcopal Church.* Author, Jenifer Gamber. Publisher, Church Publishing, Inc., 2006.

1. Saying one prayer for the cross and another for the invitatory bead, such as the Trisagion: "In the Name of God the Father, Son, and Holy Spirit, Amen."
2. Using the Trisagion for both the invitatory and cruciform beads.
3. Praying the Jesus Prayer for each of the seven week beads: "Lord Jesus Christ, Son of God, have mercy on me, a sinner."

As you move through the circle, repeating these prayers, you may choose to complete three full rounds—symbolizing the Trinity of Father, Son, and Holy Spirit. Gamber notes that by the end of three cycles, you will have prayed one hundred times. More importantly, your heart will be still, and your mind at rest. Before concluding, spend a moment in silent gratitude, acknowledging God's presence.

The Role of Breath in Prayer

Another essential aspect of this practice is our breath. Let your focus on your breathing during either of these practices remind you that God is closer to you than even your own breath. Let your breath draw you back into your body, reduces stress, and slow your heart rate. The body, as the dwelling place of God, reflects the diversity and beauty of creation.

I pray that this book serves as a humble offering to leaders, clergy, and anyone seeking trauma-informed religious spaces. Together, let us work toward a ministry that honors healing, embodiment, and sacred presence.

PART 1

Chapter 1

Meaning-Making
as a Path to Healing

> Trauma is not what happens to you, but what
> happens inside you as a result of what happens
> to you.
>
> —Gabor Maté

Purity Culture and Spiritual Trauma

I once encountered the assertion that the trauma of "purity culture" can rival the wounds left by sexual abuse. I can't pinpoint where I read this, nor can I claim it as an established truth. When I say "purity culture," I refer to a socioreligious movement, primarily within evangelical Christianity, that emphasizes sexual abstinence before marriage and strict adherence to traditional gender roles. In the most destructive settings, this purity was directly linked to one's worth and worthiness before God. Perhaps you read books such as *I Kissed Dating Goodbye* by Joshua Harris or books on strict gender roles by John and Elizabeth Eldridge. My youth pastor encouraged me to read such books. How else would I know what to look for in a husband?

Conservatism blanketed my upbringing, serving as a tight grip that shielded me from what I can only assume were the dangers of sexuality. In the early 2000s, when I was coming of age, my parents seemed most concerned about the emotional risk of having sex. And so, I was withdrawn from age-appropriate health education in those late elementary-school years, an act rooted in fear of what some term "abortionism," a phrase laden with a heavy weight that bore down on my young mind. Eventually, I was pulled out of school entirely to focus on a homeschool model that left me less educated in my high school years than most kids my age.

In middle or high school (I can't recall which anymore), I was in a dimly lit youth room, separated by gender, where a youth leader wielded an unsettling metaphor. He produced a piece of packaging tape, drawing a parallel between it and my virginity. "This piece of tape," he declared, "represents your purity. Giving your virginity away lightly is like sticking it to someone else's arm." He pressed the tape down, then tore it away. "See how it loses its stickiness? Each time you try to adhere it elsewhere, it loses more until it can't stick."

Even at my young age, the absurdity of the analogy was not lost on me. Yet, that vivid image—of tape rendered useless—seeped into my adolescent psyche. Purity culture ultimately colored everything we talked about in the community in which I grew up.

The message I received, even if unintentionally, was that God would stop liking or loving me depending on what I did or did not do. And this is simply not the case. Today I have come to notice that many of our collects and prayers begin with "Gracious God," and it was only until after I repeated this phrase consistently that I realized that God was truly gracious to those around me. Still, if you had asked me if God was gracious toward *me*, I had trouble believing it for myself. It was not until more recently that I began to own that I was worthy of God's grace simply for being human. And I want anyone who reads this work to understand that God's grace is for them as well.

Grace, Worthiness, and Healing

I share this religious trauma first because I want those who have experienced the feeling of being inadequate of God's grace to feel less alone. And this story isn't really about what happened *to me*; it's a story about how it affected my inner life and what I came to believe about myself and about God. Was God just a dictator in the sky telling me what I could and couldn't do? Hearing this type of teaching on my growing adolescent mind from those who are supposed to spiritually mentor me had a lasting impression upon me. An impression that I did unlearn but perhaps shouldn't have had to unlearn.

In another example, I've read firsthand accounts of the deeply damaging impacts of conversion therapy upon gay youth, a prominent practice in the '90s but which is still practiced in some conservative Christian churches today. Some scholars have written that conversion therapy can be considered a form of torture. The most easily accessible example comes from an independent expert for the United Nations, Victor Madrigal-Borloz, who came out with a report arguing for a worldwide ban of the practice.[1]

It's because of my background that I see the world through the lens of trauma and how to liberate ourselves from it. I believe these stories can ground those who suffer in other people's resilience, leaving behind any kind of shame for the abuse they did not deserve. And it's in these most raw and genuine stories one can start to appreciate our shared common humanity. But even more than that, the *meaning we humans make from our histories of trauma* might be one of the most determinative factors in our resilience.

---

1   "'Conversion Therapy' Can Amount to Torture and Should Be Banned Says UN Expert," United Nations Office of the High Commissioner for Human Rights, July 13, 2020, https://www.ohchr.org/en/stories/2020/07/conversion-therapy-can-amount-torture-and-should-be-banned-says-un-expert.

The Biology of Trauma

I want to elevate the words of Dr. Peter A. Levine, a professional in the field of trauma studies, who explains that trauma responses, at their most basic level, come down to human biology. He explains that trauma taps into the deep reptilian part of the human brain that is essential to all animals, including humans. According to Levine, trauma responses are part of God's design, as it ensures the survival of a species and is the body's way of searching to survive. If we can understand our human reptilian brains we can evolve our thinking from which all higher intelligence has evolved.[2]

Such an understanding can help normalize trauma as a human fact of life. Every human being has some form of past trauma. This fact can bind us together in our humanity and brokenness. When we consider various trauma responses as part of the essential human experience, and in moments of distress, our reptilian brain.

From one point of view, perhaps we can understand that Christ, being fully human, seemed to have experienced these same reptilian responses. Scripture tells us that Jesus wept, retreated to a mountaintop in solitude, and asked God to take the burden of death on a cross away from him. The Gospels

2   Peter A. Levine and Ann Frederick, *Waking the Tiger: Healing Trauma: The Innate Capacity to Transform Overwhelming Experiences* (North Atlantic, 1997), 33–42.

are chock-full of what Christ did in the face of significant trauma and suffering.

So often, however, we repress the effects of our own traumas. Perhaps you can relate to stuffing down the impact of a traumatic instance and ignoring it until it bursts forth without any guardrails. In reality, a trauma response is nothing to be ashamed of; instead, it is expected and can be faced head-on with authenticity, bravery, and honesty. Current responses to past trauma are simply a mechanism of our brain looking for danger and seeking survival. For better or for worse, many of these processes take place in the mind's unconscious. A supportive religious community can offer space to bring the unconscious into the conscious mind. *How* we bring the unconscious forward is the main topic of this book.

No one wants to be forced to bring their unconscious trauma forward, and pushing this process along can even be harmful. All persons must be individually ready to face their trauma when the time is right for them. To that end, consent is an essential factor in a healthy discussion about trauma.[3] So, how do clergy and lay leaders create a safe place to foster God's healing instead of contributing to environments that cause harm?

Understanding collective trauma is a great starting point. Obvious examples of collective trauma from American

---

3   More on this, including resources for garnering consent in discussion groups or private conversations, will be outlined in a later chapter.

history may include Pearl Harbor, Jonestown, 9/11, and most recently, the COVID-19 pandemic. A preeminent if not foundational work on collective trauma is by Kai Erikson, who in the 1970s wrote about the Buffalo Creek Flood and its impact on the social fabric of the larger community. However, even in the case of collective trauma, I contend that the effects of that trauma will have a unique imprint on each of us. It's unique because we each carried, processed, and faced this societal trauma differently. And it's unique in large part because of the social-racial-economic differences or disparities.

Collective trauma offers a helpful starting point because it is a shared and relatable experience among parishioners. Throughout this book, I often refer to the pandemic as a grounding example for thinking about trauma and healing. I focus on this particular collective trauma because it has some distance from us now, and, hopefully, the wounds it left have begun to heal. Over time, you may find that such collective traumatic events become easier to reflect on and discuss.

So using the pandemic as a case study, let's consider how each person has their own traumas *and* privileges. An online creator I follow coined the term "traum-lidges," which combines these two words.[4] This term recognizes that when one speaks about trauma, one might also consider one's

---

4   White Woman Whisperer, at https://www.whitewomanwhisperer.com/.

privileges. This is another way to speak about wide disparities in our modern world.

Privilege and trauma intertwined in the life of a close clergy friend, who graciously agreed to share their story with me for this project. During the COVID-19 pandemic, they were hospitalized in a psychiatric facility for three weeks over Thanksgiving 2020, in part due to short-term clergy burnout.

In the midst of this deeply personal crisis, my friend shared a hope: that their experience of encountering both trauma and privilege simultaneously might become clearer to others engaging in this kind of work. Throughout their hospital stay, I reached out to them daily. I wasn't able to visit in person, and their family was not permitted to either, due to necessary COVID restrictions. The absence of familiar faces—their core support system—was excruciating. I watched from a distance as their mind struggled to stay tethered to reality. I couldn't help but imagine how many others in similar positions must have felt equally isolated and alone. Even for those who weren't hospitalized, we can all remember how deeply the pandemic's isolation impacted us.

As I observed my friend's journey, I often felt helpless—a bystander to their suffering. Isn't that often the reality of pastoral ministry? We accompany, observe, and witness the human journey more than we fix or solve it. I witnessed the toll of necessary medications, the indignity of a shared bedroom with no privacy, and the fragility of their mental state. Their once lively, enthusiastic spirit seemed unrecognizable at times, and often I found myself at a loss for words. It felt as if the hospitalization itself was a kind of unique prison—almost custom-made to break a thoughtful, vibrant clergy person.

Afterward, my friend recounted their experience: the crushing boredom, the endless days without family visits, outdoor time, or programming—all casualties of COVID restrictions. Yet, in the aftermath, they shared a profound realization. Despite the trauma, they had a job they loved, a supportive family, and a beautiful home waiting for them. Others they met during that time were facing far harsher realities: no homes, no family support, and no clear path forward. Through witnessing their experience, I came to see how privilege accompanies us even in the midst of trauma. Having a robust support system—family, friends, access to clinicians—can make a significant difference in recovery and healing.

One thing my friend emphasized was that, during their hospital stay, they didn't think about God. Instead, they remembered asking a middle-aged floor manager to play chess—a simple but profound search for companionship in an isolating environment. They didn't engage in their usual spiritual practices: no journaling, no drawing, no Bible reading—highly uncharacteristic for them. For a time, they believed God had abandoned them. Exhausted, they wrestled with their own mind: *Maybe if I sleep more, this won't happen again. How can I get out of here? I need to get out now.*

And yet, today, I have no doubt that God was with them. When I recently sat down with them, I asked if they could now look back and see God's presence in those friendships and small moments of connection. They told me that only recently had they begun to see that season in a new light.

As Christians, we believe that Christ is fully present with us—even, and especially, in our suffering. Looking back, my friend now takes comfort in knowing Christ was present even in the awful sounds of the hospital unit, in the loneliness, and in the despair. Though they couldn't perceive it at the time, God was there. Reflecting on that season has helped my friend unpack the experience, knowing now that their mental health crisis did not separate them from God. In many ways, it drew them closer, affirming the deep truth that God fully understands and lovingly embraces every part of our human journey.

In his book on pastoral responses to the problem of evil, John Swinton says, "First there is pain, then there is reflection."[5] He argues that the problem of evil cannot be separated from people's real experiences. One shouldn't jump too quickly to the stage of reflection, but reflection is part of the healing process. Much of this chapter is about how to reflect on the experiences of darkness one may have had. Ultimately, pain and healing coexist in a complex and beautiful way, just as trauma and privilege intermingle as well.

---

5   John Swinton, *Raging with Compassion*, 16.

Importance of Self-Care for Clergy

Nowhere does this complexity of pain and healing exist more acutely than in pastoral ministry. In many ways we are living in unprecedented times. Trauma from our very own government is rampant. We may be wondering if another global pandemic is just around the corner or if some of our basic rights might be taken away. Others fear deportation and struggle to feel safe anywhere. And yet, as priests and pastors, we are called to come alongside those who suffer. If I'm completely honest, walking alongside traumatized individuals can be wearying. For those who relate, sometimes my empathetic personality becomes overwhelmed and consumed with the suffering I see in the world. It puts me into a paralyzed state, and I seize up when I try to think about where to begin. I have a few exercises and reflection activities to support our ministry for traumatized individuals, but I'm getting ahead of myself.

Many clergypersons carry the weight of their parishioners' pain. Fundamentally, this kind of empathy is commendable and critical to healing trauma. Clergypersons have the chance to offer validation to God's people. And yet, clergypersons coming into contact with a variety of traumatized individuals must find respite in order to self-regulate and maintain spiritual care for others.

I want to encourage you to take a moment to write down what gives you life. And what is a life without joy and humor?

I'll be honest with you: I don't usually find much humor in day-to-day work, but I'm profoundly unserious at my core! I regularly use my access to technology to enjoy comedians and other funny creators who bring me joy. Even in the darkest of nights, one should never deny one's body a chance to laugh from the belly! I truly believe that laughter is some of the best medicine and the highest form of resistance; while it may not heal your mind or body, it certainly plays a role in healing the soul.

Tip:

For those leading congregations—especially solo priests or pastors—remember that you're not meant to do this work alone! I encourage you to start compiling a list of trusted resources within your community. Begin by asking parishioners for recommendations, such as therapists, psychiatrists, or social workers whose work they trust.

Additionally, consider including advocacy groups and community organizations that can offer specialized support. This might include the National Alliance for Mental Illness (NAMI), natural-disaster-preparedness groups, and other local organizations that address the unique needs of your community. Having a well-rounded list of reliable resources can empower you to better support your parishioners and meet diverse needs effectively.

The various activities or hobbies that bring you the most joy can also be considered your coping skills. Coping skills can help you support your journey with traumatized individuals by maintaining proper self-care that combats weariness. Take a moment to write out a list of activities that bring you joy.

Here is my list of things I do to get my ideas flowing for how to take care of myself so that I can care for those before me:

Ways Clergy Can Avoid Burnout

1. **Engage in Music**
   - Playing or listening to music can be a powerful way to relieve stress and reconnect with joy.
   - Making music with others fosters community, creativity, and emotional expression.
   - Consider learning an instrument, singing in a choir, or simply curating playlists that uplift your spirit.

2. **Prioritize Physical Movement**
   - Exercise helps regulate the body's stress response, especially when experiencing prolonged ministry-related pressure.
   - Activities like walking, stretching, or dancing can release tension and promote overall well-being.
   - If feeling overwhelmed, a short walk outdoors or a gentle yoga session can reset your nervous system.

3. **Maintain a Tidy and Peaceful Space**
   ○ A clutter-free environment can create mental clarity and reduce anxiety.
   ○ Cleaning and organizing can be a mindful, grounding practice.
   ○ Consider setting small, achievable cleaning goals to create a sense of order without feeling overwhelmed.

4. **Engage in Handcrafts or Creative Hobbies**
   ○ Activities like crocheting, knitting, painting, or woodworking help you stay present and cultivate a sense of accomplishment.
   ○ Creativity engages the brain in a restorative way, offering a break from problem-solving and pastoral responsibilities.

5. **Spend Time with Pets**
   ○ Animals provide comfort, companionship, and an opportunity to practice care outside of ministry duties.
   ○ Walking a dog, stroking a cat, or simply watching pets play can be incredibly grounding.

6. **Make Space for Play and Imagination**
   ○ Engaging in playful activities, especially with children, reignites joy and lightheartedness.
   ○ Laughter and imagination can be powerful antidotes to stress.

○ Try board games, storytelling, or even unstructured time to explore creativity.

7. **Connect with Nature**

○ Walking on the beach, hiking in the woods, or simply sitting in a park can help you feel God's presence in creation.

○ Fresh air and natural beauty have been shown to lower stress and enhance overall well-being.

○ Consider scheduling regular outdoor retreats, even if just for a short walk.

8. **Practice Meditation and Stillness**

○ Meditation helps regulate the parasympathetic nervous system, reducing stress and promoting inner balance.

○ Simple practices like deep breathing, centering prayer, or mindful silence can bring clarity and peace.

○ Even five minutes of stillness a day can help ground you in God's presence.

9. **Journal for Reflection and Processing**

○ Writing helps verbalize emotions, process experiences, and find deeper meaning in ministry.

○ Journaling about gratitude, struggles, or spiritual insights can provide a much-needed outlet for personal growth.

○ Consider starting a simple daily or weekly journaling practice to track emotions and reflections.

10. **Set Healthy Boundaries**
    - Ministry can be all-consuming, but setting limits is essential for sustainability.
    - Learn to say no when necessary and protect time for rest, family, and personal growth.
    - Regularly evaluate your commitments to prevent overextension.

11. **Seek Support and Community**
    - Clergy often carry the burdens of others—having a support system is crucial.
    - Engage with trusted mentors, fellow clergy, or a therapist for guidance and encouragement.
    - Spiritual direction can offer a sacred space for personal and vocational discernment.

I invite you to use this space
below to write your own list of coping skills

_____

_____

_____

_____

_____

_____

_____

As a child, I didn't realize that playing my viola was a critical coping skill. I would spend hours poring over fingerings, practicing vibrato, and replaying passages. It wasn't until much later in my life that I realized having a creative outlet like this was a way for me to cope with my own trauma and challenges. I still play music in a local orchestra to care for my soul. Being emotionally and physically present within my own musical expressions and being part of this music-making community offers a chance to be present within my own body, present in the moment at hand. I've come to recognize how relaxed I feel after spending two-and-a-half hours rehearsing challenging pieces of music. For you, it may be movement or some other creative outlet.

Many of these suggestions may seem like simple or easy steps, but empathy burnout is a real experience. If you have a gift and a heart for traumatized individuals, please prioritize your own self-care in these crucial times of trauma healing. Denying yourself the things you need to stay nourished and rooted in God's love doesn't help anyone and especially doesn't help you.

Keep your list of creative and fulfilling activities visible, and I'd suggest that church leaders engage in at least one life-giving activity every day, wholly separate from your care for traumatized individuals. Ultimately, the goal is to remain detached enough so that another person's trauma does not trigger you or become your own. It's a form of self-protection in this work as we walk alongside folks from varied backgrounds.

Narrative Identity and the Healing Power of Storytelling

Another reason why deep community is so significant in trauma healing is that it is not unusual for a person on the outside to pick up on biological trauma responses before that individual can name or identify it for themselves. This insight into one's ability to process trauma can be helpful to clergy when navigating complex group dynamics or individual spiritual care because you might see an instinctual trauma response before the person can articulate its full scope in their life.

Dr. Shelley Rambo, author of *Spirit and Trauma* and *Resurrecting Wounds*, puts it this way: "In the aftermath of trauma . . . one's access to language and the ability to communicate with others is profoundly affected."[6] She goes on to emphasize that the ability of an individual to put their trauma response into words is deeply affected by the brain's instinctual response when a person is in a situation that alerts the mind and the body to imminent danger. It's almost as if, in a traumatic moment, the brain has to prioritize its own survival, so language falls by the wayside.

---

6   Rambo, *Spirit and Trauma*, 18.

The subconscious phenomenon at play when a person has difficulty accessing language post-trauma provides a window into why sharing stories is critical to the healing process. Northwestern University psychologist Dan McAdams is an expert in a concept he calls "narrative identity." His work relies on the core principle that humans are storytelling beings. Perhaps you can recall the stories you told yourself in adolescence and see how those stories have impacted or changed your point of view now as an adult. This is an example of a narrative identity. According to McAdams, "narrative identities reconstruct the autobiographical past and anticipate the imagined future to provide the self with temporal coherence and some semblance of psychosocial unity and purpose."[7] For instance, I know I have much more "temporal coherence" now, in my midthirties, about my own adolescence.

In another article about McAdams's work, Emily Esfahani Smith puts it this way:

> Our identities and experiences are constantly shifting, and story-telling is how we make sense of it. By taking the disparate pieces of our lives and placing them together into a narrative, we create a unified whole that allows us to understand our lives as coherent—and coherence, psychologists say, is a key source of meaning.[8]

---

7   McAdams, "First We Invented Stories," 2.
8   Smith, "Two Kinds of Stories."

I have personally found healing in articulating my journey through trauma. I find that I can even measure or understand a given point in time better when I articulate my journey through that trauma. I can understand where I am in the larger narrative of my life. I can begin to understand where I am in this journey of healing. My journal holds many secrets! But articulating my "secrets" helped me to know where I am in my healing journey. I can tell from how I talk about something and how an emotion bubbles up whether I'm ready to share my story with the broader world or even just a small parish. I can tell if my trauma is still speaking first or if the healing is speaking first. It sounds nebulous, but after sixteen-plus years of personal trauma therapy, I can usually identify where my mind and body are in relationship to a traumatic event. It has significantly influenced how I've found psychosocial unity and purpose.

Here is another way to think about it. Consider everything that has ever happened to you as the "text" of your life. One can exegete the places where one has seen God show up in one's life. Those are the places that are worth your deeper exploration. Just as you may exegete the Holy Scriptures for God's presence as you try to glean meaning from them, you can exegete your own life as a living human document. That is not to say your own life replaces the role of Holy Scripture. That is just to say that you can use the same exegetical muscle memory when untangling trauma.

In that same vein, priests and pastors often have the authority in their religious communities to uplift certain stories. One practical possibility is for such leaders to find spaces to uplift those who have made their way through the journey of trauma healing. Offer them a public space to share their reflections if they so desire. One parish I served in hosted a time called "A Living Epistle." A living epistle is a play upon the biblical genre of letters written to groups of the earliest Christians. A living epistle can be offered in any context that feels most appropriate in your community. Some of the questions they might answer could include:

1. How did your spirituality help you through a difficult season?[9]
2. Who came around you to support you during that time? Why were they so important to your story?
3. What meaning did you find either during or after a difficult season?

---

9   Notice I have used the phrase "difficult season" instead of "trauma." You will need to decide how your community will receive that precise language of "trauma" and which phrasing will be more productive in your context.

Tip:

Gathering people to share their experiences from the pandemic—
or any collective trauma, such as a natural disaster, mass shooting,
or other significant event—can be a powerful opportunity for
storytelling, reflection, and community healing. These gatherings
can even serve as a kind of "Living Epistle," where the stories
shared become a living testimony of resilience and grace.

Consider creating a safe, intentional space where participants feel
empowered to share their experiences authentically. Whether
reflecting on personal challenges or celebrating small victories,
these conversations can foster deep connection and provide a
pathway toward communal healing.

Let me be clear: I'm not here to say that God always teaches
us a lesson in a traumatic experience. In fact, I decidedly do
not believe *everything happens for a reason.* There exists such a
thing as pointless suffering, purposeless suffering, suffering for
the sake of suffering, and nothing else. (Genocide is the most
obvious example of purposeless suffering.) However, humans
are meaning-making beings. We long for meaning in the midst
of our pain. Oftentimes, there is spiritual relief in voicing the
meaning one has made from one's own trauma. This process
of making meaning is just as subjective and diverse as all of
humanity. At various points in a person's life, they may have
one sense of meaning compared to another point in their life.

There isn't necessarily a right and wrong answer to whatever meaning you make of a given trauma. Part of the clerical imperative is helping others to decipher what is true for them.

The world-renowned psychiatrist and physician Gabor Maté suffered excruciating trauma as an infant in Nazi Germany. In an interview with the Skoll Foundation, he says, "Trauma is not what happens *to you*, it's what happens *inside* you . . . the wound that you sustained, the meaning you made of it, the way you then came to believe certain things about yourself."[10] This powerful reframing takes back the ability to articulate a narrative identity around one's trauma. The suffering itself isn't the point, even while some people may be captivated by the gruesome details of one's trauma. I hear Maté arguing that the gruesome details are not the point. At first, the meaning you make from a traumatic instance might be different than the meaning you derive from it much later in your life. Maté's words are an important reminder that making meaning from one's trauma is a critical part of any process of healing. Ultimately, this understanding offers greater agency to the traumatized!

Understanding Trauma Responses

What does a possible trauma response look like? This biological understanding will help clergy identify various human behaviors around the effects of trauma. When we as clergy

---

10   Maté, Gabor, and Daniel Maté. *The Myth of Normal: Trauma, Illness, and Healing in a Toxic Culture.* New York: Avery, 2022.

and religious leaders can have a greater understanding of human behavior as it relates to trauma, we can glean bits of information from our conversations that may be helpful as we navigate these spaces with the parishioners we serve.

Most physicians and psychiatrists agree that there are four main responses to trauma. Importantly, you should remember that these are instinctual, and Pete Walker, in *Complex PTSD: From Surviving to Thriving* reminds us that a complex nervous system is behind these responses. These responses are hardly voluntary. And there is still so much we don't know about the human brain and trauma. However, Walker outlines the four responses.

Fight

The fight response is activated when an individual perceives a threat and reacts with aggression or confrontation as a means of self-preservation. This doesn't necessarily mean physical violence—it can also manifest as arguing, defensiveness, controlling behavior, or even an intense need to assert dominance. This response is rooted in the belief that overcoming or overpowering the threat is the best way to ensure safety.

Flight

The flight response occurs when a person perceives danger and instinctively reacts by escaping, avoiding, or withdrawing from the situation. This could be a literal response—such as running away or leaving a stressful environment—or a psychological one, like excessive busyness, avoidance of confrontation, or an overwhelming urge to remove oneself from perceived danger. This response is driven by the need to find safety through distance.

Freeze

The freeze response happens when the brain determines that resistance or escape is impossible or too dangerous. The person may feel stuck, numb, or disconnected from reality, sometimes experiencing dissociation or emotional shutdown. This response is similar to how animals "play dead" to avoid predation—it is a survival mechanism that minimizes attention and reduces the chance of further harm.

Fawn

The fawn response is a survival strategy where a person instinctively attempts to appease a perceived threat by being overly accommodating, helpful, or people-pleasing. This response often develops in environments where confrontation or resistance feels unsafe, leading the person to prioritize the needs of others over their own in an effort to avoid conflict or harm.

These four responses are automatic, deeply ingrained survival mechanisms designed to protect individuals from real or perceived danger. However, when triggered in everyday situations that are not truly life-threatening, they can contribute to patterns of stress, anxiety, and difficulty in relationships. Recognizing these responses can be a crucial step toward healing and self-awareness.[11]

To use a social example, think about your own trauma responses during the COVID-19 shutdown. This journaling exercise is designed to give you space to engage with your past and perhaps glean some new insight by retelling your own story. Did you fight, flee, freeze, or fawn?

Tip:

An open sharing circle can be a powerful space for healing, but it requires thoughtful planning and care. I strongly encourage any leader considering hosting a sharing circle to review the recommendations I provide later in this book. One significant risk for trauma survivors is the possibility of oversharing, which can leave them feeling vulnerable or exposed. To prevent this, consent is essential—participants should share only if they feel genuinely compelled to do so.

When creating these spaces, it's crucial to be discerning and intentional to ensure they remain safe and supportive. I've included a comprehensive guide with practical suggestions for facilitating safe small groups and discussion circles. I highly recommend reviewing these guidelines in chapter 2 before hosting storytelling circles or similar gatherings.

---

11 Pete Walker, *Complex PTSD*, 13.

I'd encourage you to think about how COVID-19
impacted your life and take a minute to answer these questions
in the journaling space below. I have intentionally worded
these questions to reduce any sense of shame. Remember,
these four Fs are natural responses in moments of trauma and
have become tools for our brains and bodies to cope in the
moment. There should be no shame associated with any of
these four responses, as God has created the complexity of our
brains on purpose! Given the time and space to process their
meaning, I hope you can evaluate their patterns and perhaps
revisit the traumatic moments in a new light. Perhaps you
will find a bit of narrative identity, perhaps you will discover
a trauma response you hadn't noticed at first, or perhaps you
will find meaning in your pain.

Take a moment or longer to reflect on the following questions for your own life:

1. Do you have a particular response of these four that you
   tend to lean upon in a moment of trauma? (Fight, Flight,
   Freeze, or Fawn?)
2. Did you find one of these useful during the COVID-19
   pandemic?
3. Why might this have been your tool during that time?
4. What did you miss out on by using that tool?

5. What new meaning have you discovered from that time in your life?

6. Was God present with you? If so, how? If not, why might God have felt absent to you?

_____

_____

_____

_____

_____

_____

_____

_____

_____

_____

_____

_____

_____

_____

_____

_____

_____

_____

_____

_____

Chapter 2

Grounding Grace
and Holding Space

> Though we do not wholly believe it yet, the interior life is a real life, and the intangible dreams of people have a tangible effect on the world.
>
> —James Baldwin

Introduction: Trauma and Spirit

As Christians, we are an Easter people. But perhaps, like me, we are too quick to move from death straight to resurrection. Historically, Christians have spent less time with the liminal space between death and resurrection. However, it is during the time between Christ's death and resurrection when we witness the ultimate journey from trauma to life. I recognize the need to dwell within Holy Saturday, where trauma lingers, in order to see how the Spirit of God works in moments that we think are hopeless.

Shelley Rambo reminds us to resist the urge to rush from Good Friday's trauma to Easter Sunday's triumph. The Synoptic Gospels are silent about Holy Saturday. But, as Rambo argues in *Spirit and Trauma*, the middle day, Holy Saturday, demonstrates a more complex relationship between death and life. This complex relationship is precisely what Rambo sets out to examine.

I've noticed something uncomfortable about healing trauma—something I'm nervous to admit. Sometimes, when someone lays their raw, aching pain before me, I feel a reflexive resistance. It's not that I don't care, but in that moment, someone's trauma feels too heavy, too sharp, too close to something buried in me. My heart quickens, and my body tenses up, and before I know it, I'm pulling back, grasping for a lifeline to safety. I rush to solutions or silver linings, eager to skip ahead to resurrection and redemption. Eager, too keen, to retreat. But in doing so, I think we— myself included—miss the actual assignment. Namely, it is important to stand in solidarity with those who suffer.

In this chapter, I will offer a series of self-reflective exercises designed to help us dwell a little longer in the tension of Holy Saturday. Through these practices, I invite you to resist the urge to rush through the discomfort of unresolved trauma, for it is not in bypassing the pain but in bearing witness to what remains of trauma that genuine healing can begin.

Witness and Grief

Through the eyes of Mary Magdalene, Rambo explores the movement of the Spirit within the Holy Saturday narrative of the Johannine gospel. After Christ dies and has been buried within the tomb, the apostles lose hope. Many board themselves up in a private room, fearing the consequences of following a man who was condemned to death by the Romans. During the time between the death and resurrection of Jesus, there is an air of hopelessness, of desperation, of loss. I can only imagine what they were going through, having lost their rabbi and Lord, but this sorrow—this grief—only made Mary's *witness*—her witnessing of trauma—more powerful.

Let's overlay some of the concepts about trauma that have already been discussed. Consider my previous mentions of how language can fail us in the aftermath of trauma. Mary didn't yet have the words, and she didn't yet understand who this figure was walking out of the tomb. It certainly couldn't be Jesus, whom she previously saw beaten, carrying the cross, with a crown of thorns pressed into his brow.

John 20:1 tells us she comes to the tomb while it is still dark, both literally and metaphorically. She is walking through the darkness of her own grief, her vision clouded by loss and confusion. The text tells us the stone is rolled away, but it's unclear if Mary fully understands what she is seeing. As Rambo notes, her witness is dominated by unseeing, by an inability to fully comprehend or locate what is before her.[1] Rambo suggests that instead of seeing Mary's tears as penitence, we should see them as grief. And grief can obscure our language, our seeing, our decision making, and our understanding.

There is hope in remaining with Mary at the tomb. But this hope doesn't erase the wounds, scars, and marks of trauma. Just as the Resurrection doesn't remove the wounds, trauma does not simply disappear. Even the disciples ask to see Jesus's scars after he is raised, and he shows them. Even in his glorified body, Christ's wounds remain.

One of the most striking moments in Mary's story is what Rambo calls "The Turning Problem."[2] In John 20:14, Mary turns toward Jesus but does not recognize him. It is only after he calls her by name that she turns again and sees him for who he is. This moment is crucial, not only for what it says about Mary's recognition of Christ, but for what it teaches us about witness. Recognition, Rambo argues, is not dependent on sight alone. It is relational. It happens when we are called, when we are named, and when we remain open to the possibility of encounter.

1   Rambo, *Spirit and Trauma*, 85.
2   Rambo, *Spirit and Trauma*, 87.

What is clear from this biblical story is that it takes great courage to engage with what remains. No matter what level is most fitting, trauma on a personal level or trauma within a religious community, it all takes great bravery to address head-on. I want to leave you with a few more practical concepts that may be critical in these spaces.

As we navigate personal and societal traumas, like those brought to the surface during the COVID-19 pandemic, embracing the invitation of Holy Saturday becomes essential. It is here, in the messy, unresolved middle, that we begin to understand the depth of Christ's Resurrection and its transformative power in our own lives. Trauma may remain, but so does grace. And that changes everything.

Grounding In Grace

This work is messy and difficult and, sometimes, there are twists and turns that we don't expect. Writing about something like trauma is a bit like trying to write about all the points of view in the entire world all at once. But, my friend, you are here. *We* are here. And you set aside some time to think about trauma. Maybe your own. Maybe for the parishioners you care for. Most likely, a little bit of both.

Before diving into the practical tools of healing, let us first ground ourselves in the grace that makes such work possible, a grace that interrupts trauma and invites restoration. Our faith speaks to us about an unconditional grace. A grace that is set apart for the whole of humanity. A grace that interrupts the very patterns of violence that invade our minds and hearts in a polarized society. It's God's grace that can interrupt those patterns of violence or felt trauma. God's grace comes in many shapes, sizes, and forms. Sometimes, it's a great psychological team of doctors; other times, it's a validating community; other times, it's sharing in laughter with a good group of friends.

The parish setting is not the only way to interrupt those patterns of felt trauma. It can be one place to dismantle and reheal from a traumatic experience. Ultimately, we cannot conjure up this kind of love by ourselves; we can only receive it and do our best to offer what we have received in Christ to those in our midst.

Grounding oneself in grace is not just a theological concept, theoretical and lofty. But we also live it out in our embodied spiritual rituals. Let me turn us toward some examples of embodied rituals.

Embodied Rituals

The Christian tradition is rich with embodied expressions. An embodied ritual allows the mind-body relationship to be healed—a vital reconnection after the disconnection trauma often causes. Spiritual rituals can be personal and private, as well as corporate and collective.

Let me give you a few examples. I came to the Episcopal Church as a hired minister but also as a bit of an outsider because I was ordained in a different denomination. I remember those first few weeks in the parish well—how I studied the rhythms of the liturgy and listened closely to the language of the prayers, trying to find my place within it all. It was an interesting season, not only because I was learning but because the parish itself had an openness, a willingness to embrace new ideas. They welcomed my perspective and gave me space to bring creativity into our worship.

One of my boldest suggestions was to embrace a community art project, or a collective artistic project, as part of the liturgy. This may, at first, sound unconventional. However, I imagined a moment where worship, creativity, and expression would intertwine, where hands and hearts could physically participate in something beautiful. So, one Sunday, after folks received the Eucharist, they stepped down into the crossing of the sanctuary where a blank canvas with a large outline of a cross lay in the center along with an array of paints.

At first, there was hesitation. A few curious glances. I thought I might have heard someone whisper, "Are we really allowed to do this?" I even thought it to myself as well. But slowly, one by one, they dipped their thumbs into vibrant blues, deep reds, and warm yellows, pressing them onto the canvas. Soon, at the center, a halo of color surrounded the symbol of Christ's cross, thumbprints of the faithful surrounded it—a living testament to our shared life together.

It became more of a symbol of community than I had even anticipated.

As I watched, my understanding of shared community was beginning to take shape. The sacred was in the bread and wine but it was also in this act of creation, in the smudges of paint left by young and old alike, the able-bodied and the differently abled. This, I realized, was community. This made our faith embodied, tangible, and tactile. It became an image that we could all look back on and remember collectively.

Let me share another one of my favorite personal sensory activities, which I return to often. During a particularly overwhelming season of the pandemic, one of the best pieces of advice I received from a doctor was deceptively simple: hold a frozen orange. At first, I was hesitant to try it out, but when I did, I didn't regret it.

When I hold a frozen orange, the cold sensation tells my senses to awaken. No matter how detached I am, it forces me to return to my body and the present moment. I pay attention to the texture of the orange under my fingertips, bumpy and uneven. The scent of a frozen orange is also soothing. Wafts of citrus fill my nostrils and calm my brain.

This simple orange—cold, fragrant, but alive in my hands—becomes a prayer. In its weight and texture, I feel grounded by God's creation, a reminder that I am part of something larger. It's as if God whispers through this orange: "Be still. Be here. Be you." I now keep a frozen orange in my freezer at all times. The simplicity of holding a part of God's creation within my own hands, an orange, has become a spiritual ritual for me.

Yet, for others, a mind-body ritual may be the ancient tradition of signing the cross, starting with the forehead, chest, left side, and right side. Many Christians now practice this sign regularly as a benediction over our bodies and persons. However, the earliest forms of signation can be traced to ancient Judaism. Hatchett says, "In Judaism, the newly baptized person was branded as God's sheep, slave, and soldier by being marked on the forehead with the Taw (T), the last letter of the alphabet, signifying the name of God."[3] The apostolic tradition of Hippolytus Christianized this symbol and soon interpreted the symbol as a sign of the cross.[4]

This historical example has survived over millennia and is a sign we still use today. When we trace the cross over ourselves, we engage in an embodied ritual, a ritual that ties us to a long tradition, together with other Christians. However, the sign of the cross is also a physical act that invites the body to participate. An embodied ritual that reminds our very cells that we are blessed and beloved members of this one church body. Signation is more than a sign; it is a physical prayer, a seal of grace, and a declaration of unity that binds us to Christ and to one another.

---

3 Hatchett, *Commentary*, 280.
4 Hatchett, *Commentary*, 280.

I encourage you to think about a spiritual ritual you find edifying. It could be a ritual from corporate worship, such as kneeling, genuflecting, or responding aloud during the service. It could also be a simple ritual practiced in a small group or a private time of prayer. Think about what sense it appeals to. Perhaps write why this ritual is meaningful to you in regards to:

1) Sight:

_____

_____

_____

_____

_____

_____

_____

2) Sound:

_____

_____

_____

_____

_____

_____

_____

3) Taste:

_____

_____

_____

_____

_____

_____

_____

4) Smell:

_____

_____

_____

_____

_____

_____

5) Touch:

_____

_____

_____

_____

_____

_____

_____

Have you considered sharing any of these rituals with your community? Why is this ritual meaningful to you? If you don't have multisensory rituals, I strongly urge you to try one. After you find a sensory ritual that is meaningful to you, you may be able to share that with a support group or small group within your parish.

Truthfully, healing from trauma can be infectious. Telling the story and sharing your own sense of healing can be just as invigorating and life-giving to others as it is to our own souls. This is the body of Christ enacting and living in healing, which is accomplished through the work of the Spirit in our lives.

As I see it, spiritual healing through Christ is truly amazing because it isn't finite. God's healing isn't a resource that will run out. When people begin to heal their trauma through God's redemptive work in their lives, others will inevitably benefit from it. That is the kinetic energy of healing. The hope of this Christian life becomes contagious. We get to be the cycle breakers who end cycles of shame, violence, and fear.

As we remain with Mary near the tomb, so too are we called to remain with the traumas that touch our communities. In the next section, I want to walk you through an example of political trauma. Political trauma is an increasing phenomenon due to the polarized nature of American and global politics. It can be felt on all sides and points of the political spectrum. This discussion is meant not to be partisan but to draw attention to the real experiences that some parishioners will inevitably understand very deeply.

Naming and Processing Emotions

Like Mary, what we feel is intrinsically important to healing. Through Mary's tears, we glimpse her grief. But to name and nurture our own emotions can be challenging. We are called to extend this care outward, shaping parish settings that honor the tender realities of those who gather. I long to see our parishes become places of emotional and psychosocial safety for all people.

One of the ways to do this is to first begin by creating it for ourselves. Our own hearts and spirits need this safe space to feel anything that needs to be felt. If we can't do that for ourselves, then we can't offer that to others in the ways that are most needed in our world right now. The whole idea of this activity is to let yourself feel exactly what it is that you need to feel. There is no right or wrong. There is no moral value that should be placed on any emotion. In the exercise that follows, try not to overanalyze quite yet. Please give yourself the space and time you need to feel whatever emotions surface. You don't have to understand them fully. Let your body respond just as it needs to.

My example of political trauma is simple. I have chosen an example that is not mired in too much cultural conflict so as to make this section land in a pastoral way. Some readers may have very explicit examples of political trauma.

My example is technically "second-order trauma." "Second-order trauma" is trauma that hasn't happened directly to you but has impacted you in some way. This is especially relevant for pastors who have witnessed or walked alongside parishioners through trauma because of the possibility of vicarious trauma. Another common example may occur for those who follow the Gaza crisis on TikTok. The images and stories shared in these spaces were intensely heartbreaking. But our brains were never meant to absorb this much vicarious trauma all at once. And certainly not meant to witness the brutality of war at our fingertips. Another example of "second-order trauma" can be found in the police brutality videos that circulated in the wake of George Floyd's death or, for that matter, any videos of police brutality.

Resmaa Menakem, a licensed social worker, identifies "second-order trauma" as "secondary trauma" or "vicarious trauma."[5] I suspect that the impact of vicarious trauma has increased with the ubiquity of social media. Now, you can see firsthand videos of police violence, climate change, and genocide taking place through these online social networks. Any individual can use the following exercise independently. I have left journaling pages for you to engage with when the time is right for you.

---

5   Menakem, *My Grandmother's Hands*, 46.

I've centered this activity around two principles from Pete Walker's work, *Complex PTSD: From Surviving to Thriving*. Complex PTSD is a particular type of PTSD that is attuned to the emotional impact of a traumatic event. Trauma, especially trauma from childhood, has the power to reshape and reframe our cognitive processes. Complex PTSD is often attributed to severe childhood neglect, but it can come about from other circumstances too, such as a significant natural disaster or a deeply personal event. In Walker's chapter on grief, he speaks about two things: balancing feelings and emoting, and verbal ventilating.[6]

Tip:

In Pete Walker's book *Complex PTSD*, I have found a great resource for understanding my own trauma and understanding the trauma of those around me. In fact, in it, he lists fifteen techniques that can really help us unpack and face emotions that swirl around one's trauma. In my opinion, the breadth of this list is worth its weight in gold. There are different learning styles and diverse approaches, even for those whose personalities tend to experience minimal emotions. I commend this list to you and highly recommend keeping a copy of this book near for your reference.

---

6   Pete Walker, *Complex PTSD*, 236–243.

I have given you a lot of information during the course of this chapter. I want to pause for a moment to offer a journaling exercise. First, you'll want to search for an emotions wheel or a feelings wheel on any search engine.[7] When I'm in an elevated emotional state, I take out my feelings wheel and ask myself to search for what I'm feeling. It's posted in my office. I'm not being cheesy here! I like more complex wheels because they offer more language, especially when I'm still searching for the right language. I have modified this exercise from Tara Schuster's book, *Glow in the F*cking Dark*.[8] She explains that this exercise is based on the teachings of a Vietnamese Buddhist priest, Thich Nhat Hanh.

My Experience

In 2015, I was brimming with hope. Attending seminary in a battleground state, I believed—wholeheartedly—that a woman would finally take the highest office in the land. But this wasn't just about politics or policy for me, a young, first-time voter. It was deeply personal.

I was pregnant during that election cycle, my daughter growing inside me. As my body formed tiny fingers and toes, I imagined a future for her that would look different than the one I'd known, perhaps a future without glass ceilings. Much

---

7 Feelings Wheel, at https://feelingswheel.com/.
8 Schuster, *Glow in the F*cking Dark*, 35–39.

of my motivation came from what I believed about gender, dignity, and possibility.

But as the election results began to come in, my hope slipped away. I remember sitting on the couch, hands burning with anger, resting protectively over my belly. The weight of the rhetoric and the deepening division settled over me like a heavy fog.

The next day in preaching class, a Puerto Rican minister stepped into the pulpit. She didn't hold back. Her voice carried *coraje*—a righteous, ancestral fire—and a message of *comunidad* she lived and breathed. It was as if she were preaching directly to our souls. Her sermon reminded us that naming what we feel is holy work—and that resisting hateful rhetoric is part of the Christian call.

Meanwhile, the raging pregnancy hormones wouldn't relent. I wept through the entire class period, slipping out more than once, overcome with grief. A voice in my head whispered cruel questions: *What will happen now? What will this mean for my daughter's future? For my own?*

Yet my friend's message was one of hope and community in a moment of social crisis. She understood the power of solidarity—of showing up for each other—and her authentic expression gave each of us permission to feel what we needed to feel.

For me, this loss felt intimate and overwhelming. But I know each of us has lived through moments when our hopes for the world—or for ourselves—crashed against a harsh reality. Maybe for you, it was a different election. Or the pandemic. Or something entirely personal—a job loss, a death, a natural disaster, or another invisible grief.

In this next exercise, I invite you to recall a moment like that in your own life. We'll hold space together to name what surfaced, to honor it, and to feel what needs to be felt.

Feelings Wheel Example

To process my own emotions, I turned to my tried and trusted feelings wheel. You will notice three concentric circles in the feelings wheel. The emotion fear, found in the innermost circle, seemed to capture the tenseness in my chest and the reality of the moment we were living in. From there, I worked outward, naming anxiety in the next layer and, finally, inadequacy in the final layer. To understand that at the core of my being I felt, as a woman, inadequate, which brought me an emotional catharsis I didn't initially expect.

Then I asked myself: What does this inadequacy need? Looking back at the wheel, I realized I needed to feel valued. I needed value in more than one way. I needed to recognize not only that I, as a human being, held inherent value but also that my body—this vessel of experience—deserved to be listened to and valued for the truths it was trying to tell me.

I imagine these balls of emotion want to stay furled up and cause us to curl inward toward ourselves. These untouched balls of emotion can cause serious rifts within our communities and within our very beings. To unravel them, to untangle our inner lives—while scary at first—will prove to be a sacred act.

Now It's Your Turn

Journaling exercises like this can be a window into your soul. They can help you remember that emotions will not be the end of you. They are natural and even welcome, almost like bits of information, points of data, that we can use to learn about ourselves, grow in our interpersonal relationships, and, most important, foster a greater appreciation for, as well as a profound understanding of, God's grace at work in our hearts and lives.

To do the following exercise, to use a feeling to give ourselves the thing that we need, is to allow God's grace to transform our relationship to our emotions. It's these difficult emotions that are the ones where we most need God to understand a new path forward. God's love, acceptance, and message of inclusion are the only thing that keeps those tightened, furled balls of emotion from exploding in ways we will later regret.

No one is meant simply to absorb the harmful rhetoric amplified in many spaces of our world. This kind of dehumanizing rhetoric grinds down upon our souls until we no longer feel human. These thoughts and emotions need gentle nurturing in a communal and relational way.

I want to leave you with some space to journal. This is just the beginning, so take some time to answer the prompt or freewrite whatever is surfacing at this moment.

Prompt: Perhaps you can think back to a difficult election season. This is a good exercise because most of us can think of the strong emotions that surfaced during those seasons (9/11, a natural disaster, vicarious trauma, or the pandemic). You could also use a profoundly personal story. Once you have identified your traumatic situation, try to locate your emotions from that time in your life using a feelings wheel. Start with the innermost circle and work your way out. I invite you to begin to do this through journaling.

Step 1:

I notice my ___*(first emotion)*_____ and I take care of my ___*(first emotion)*_____.

I notice my ___*(second emotion)* and I take care of my *(second emotion)* _____.

I notice my ___(third emotion) and I take care of my (third emotion) _____.

Once you have done this several times, you can move on to step 2.

Step 2:

My ___(first emotion)_____ needs ___(new emotion)_____.

My ___(second emotion)_____ needs ___(new emotion)_____.

My ___(third emotion)_____ needs ___(new emotion)_____.

Tip:

If this exercise is overwhelming, just use one layer of emotions. I suggest writing about it here, too. You may find it challenging if you haven't had much practice with an exercise like this. That's okay. Just like anything in life, this may take some practice. As you follow through on the exercise and various situations arise, you may find that you can more easily identify your emotions and thought patterns.

Step 3:

Now change the wording around:

I give ___*(new emotion)*_____ to my ___ *(first emotion)*_____.

I give ___*(new emotion)*_____ to my ___ *(second emotion)*_____.

I give ___*(new , emotion)*_____ to my ___ *(third emotion)*_____.

Because I have such a rich emotional life, I like to do this multiple times, but that may not work for some people. If this feels overwhelming, just focus on one emotion to begin with. With practice, you can learn to go deeper.

Tip:

This exercise can be especially helpful during clergy care when encountering emotionally charged or triggering stories from parishioners. It can also be adapted as a guided meditation for groups, fostering deeper emotional awareness and reflection.

There are countless creative ways to incorporate this practice, and you might be surprised by how naturally younger generations engage with it. Even if the exercise feels unfamiliar or a bit forced at first, I encourage you to try it a few times on your own. The benefits of identifying and naming emotions can be profound, offering clarity and grounding both individually and communally.

Chapter 3

Covenantal Connections: Support Groups in Faith Communities

> When I say it's you I like, I'm talking about that part of you that knows that life is far more than anything you can ever see or hear or touch. That deep part of you that allows you to stand for those things without which humankind cannot survive. Love that conquers hate, peace that rises triumphant over war, and justice that proves more powerful than greed.
>
> —Fred Rogers

The Pandemic and the Need for Connection

The pandemic reshaped how we relate with one another, leaving many of us longing to connect in any way possible. For my generation and Generation Z, platforms like TikTok became a lifeline, a digital sanctuary, if you will. A digital sanctuary where stories were shared, creativity flourished, and self-expression blossomed. Many found solidarity, deep community, and new friends.

In the parish community I was serving, we found our own digital sanctuary in the form of a simple, do-it-yourself podcast that didn't aim to go viral but was made especially for our little parish. In this podcast, the clergy and lay leaders took turns interviewing various people in the community. To our great delight, parishioners, some who had known each other for decades, learned things about one another that they had never known. It brought about connection and a deeper form of relationship that we hadn't thought was possible in a time of such great isolation.

Rediscovering the Power of In-Person Community

But even with these virtual spaces, my mind began to fray under the weight of isolation. I tried to outrun the guilt I felt for not being able to handle my own thoughts. Like a candle in a gust of wind, its flame was on the verge of extinguishing. And while I blamed myself for not being able to shield the small flame, I went back to my roots.

I needed something tangible, tactile, and embodied. I rediscovered the power of old-fashioned, in-person relationships and local community groups. I couldn't hide my awkwardness at being in person with people again after so many months. I challenged myself to make eye contact, laugh with others, and choose vulnerability.

It was this experience that led me to ask: could the same kind of transformative support be cultivated in our church communities? Could the church become a place where people, whether meeting in person or online, could share their stories, find belonging, and bear one another's burdens?

Whether your parish is exploring in-person or online support groups, the foundational principles for fostering connection remain the same. Now more than ever, our congregations need spaces where people can build empathetic connections. In this chapter, I explore how support groups can help individuals process trauma, build empathy, and find belonging. By establishing clear guidelines and cultivating covenantal relationships, churches can create safe and sacred spaces where human connection becomes a transformative act of grace.

Theological Framing

As we envision the Church as a hub for social connection and healing, we don't have to reinvent the wheel. The Christian tradition offers valuable insights into how to do this. One such example comes from the World Council of Churches (WCC).

In 2024, the WCC issued a definitive statement on mental health and youth entitled "A Call for Cross-Generational Action on the Mental Health of Youth." This call to address youth mental health highlights the growing need for connection in a fragmented world. While TikTok and other digital platforms offer one way to build community, the Church is uniquely positioned to create spaces for deeper, more transformative connections. Support groups and small gatherings, where stories can be shared and heard, are tangible ways to embody Christ's call to bear one another's burdens.

There is a very clear neuroscience that supports this vision. Support groups/small groups can be impactful, and to my surprise, they go far beyond simply supporting the individuals within the group. Sharing stories of trauma has the potential to build teamwork, extend empathy, and offer belonging to the hurting. In fact, the Harvard Business Review discussed the power and effect of storytelling, explaining that humans long to share and hear one another's stories.[1] (Perhaps this is the appeal of TikTok; remember, at the time of this publication roughly 170 million Americans use this app.)

Paul Zak explains that in 2003, his lab discovered that a neurochemical called oxytocin signals in the brain whether

---

1   Paul Zak, "Why Your Brain Loves Good Storytelling," *Harvard Business Review* 28 (2014): 1–5, https://www.paladinww.com/uploads/6/5/0/8/65089471/why_your_brain_loves_good_storytelling__1_.pdf.

it's safe to approach others. Oxytocin is produced when we are trusted or shown kindness, and it motivates cooperation with others. This magical hormone ultimately enhances our sense of empathy and ability to experience others' emotions. Empathy is important—especially to humans, who are social creatures—because it "allows us to understand how others are likely to react to a situation, including those with whom we work."[2] This can begin to explain why a support circle, sharing circle, or committed small group can be effective in finding support amid a traumatic situation. Such groups help build up our empathy muscles and foster cooperation.

As mentioned earlier, a support group, healing prayer circle, sharing circle, or small group may be a valuable addition to your formation offerings, as it can have a direct impact on facing one's trauma head-on. Pete Walker reminds us that "sufficient practice with a safe enough other brings genuine experiences of comforting and restorative connection." Once again, the answer to our suffering is greater human connection. This deeper form of community serves as the connective tissue that fosters greater resilience among people from all backgrounds.

At first facilitating such a group and bringing people together can sometimes be daunting. However, in the right circumstances, parishes might be able to offer support groups,

---

2   Zak, "Storytelling." https://greatergood.berkeley.edu/article/item/how_stories _change_brain.

small groups, or other forms of verbal ventilation that are healthy and life-giving and that do not overstep our role as clergy or church leaders. Below are some of my best practices for facilitating such a group. These aren't meant as the only way to facilitate; however, for those who are beginning a small group ministry in their parishes, they may be a good starting point.

Group Guidelines

Before facing a topic such as trauma head-on in a group setting, I strongly recommend some mutually agreed-upon group guidelines to maintain important boundaries and welcome an honest conversation. Group guidelines help us honor one another and reduce situations of further harm. They can give us a framework for how to create belonging in the midst of difficult dialogue. One way to handle such guidelines is to have the group decide what is most important to them. Deciding how to be together in this journey is just as critical as the actual work of healing. Understanding the type of trauma that each person carries can bring about a stronger sense of belonging and working together.

Tip:
There are great resources from the Episcopal Church on "beloved community." Many of these principles are utilized in various curriculums and guides put out by the church. In fact, *Sojourner's* website published a very thought-provoking article in 2021 on beloved community entitled "'Beloved Community' Sounds Nice. But What Does It Mean?"[3] Depending on the context, I encourage you to start a sharing circle because it reframes safety and belonging as something we build all together with an egalitarian mindset, not a top-down mindset.

First, while participating in or facilitating a small group or sharing circle, try to refrain from advice-giving. Advice-giving is beyond the scope of the church's ability as clergy or church leaders, particularly when it comes to the messy business of trauma. We are not social workers, counselors, therapists, or psychiatrists. A sharing circle is not meant to fix someone or give advice or make suggestions about how to alleviate the pain. It's primarily about sharing unheard stories and creating belonging. The point, as mentioned in previous sections of this book, is to remain with people in possibly one of their deepest moments of need.

3 Jenna Barnett, "'Beloved Community' Sounds Nice. But What Does It Mean?" *Sojourners*, September 15, 2021, https://sojo.net/articles/beloved-community-sounds-nice-what-does-it-mean.

I recommend deciding on what community guidelines everyone in the group can agree to. As always you should feel free to make guidelines that work in your context. The National Alliance of Mental Illness (NAMI) has some great group guidelines that you can use as a starting point and that can be found on their website. The NAMI guidelines come in two categories. One is the principles of support. These can easily be modified for your context, but you can see the basic premise below. The second category is group guidelines, which are more generic, and I suspect they are more universal than even the principles of support.

Tip:

Perhaps you already have some group principles that you follow and share regularly. But if not, these NAMI guidelines can be a good starting point. I would share them with any group and ask if there are guidelines they would like to change or add.

Principles of Support:

1. We will see the individual first, not the illness.

- A person is more than their diagnosis. This principle encourages recognizing individuals for their unique qualities, strengths, and experiences rather than defining them by their mental health condition.

2. We recognize that mental illnesses are medical illnesses that may have environmental triggers.

- Mental illnesses are real medical conditions, just like diabetes or heart disease. While environmental factors (stress, trauma, or life changes) can contribute to symptoms, mental illness is not a choice, weakness, or character flaw.

3. We understand that mental illnesses are traumatic events.

- Living with a mental illness can be overwhelming and distressing. Symptoms, hospitalizations, stigma, and disruptions to daily life can be traumatic experiences that require support and healing.

4. We aim for better coping skills.

- Recovery is a journey, and learning healthy ways to cope with challenges is essential. Support groups help individuals develop strategies to manage stress, emotions, and daily struggles more effectively.

5. We find strength in sharing experiences.

- Talking about personal struggles and victories fosters connection and reduces isolation. By sharing experiences, participants inspire and support one another, creating a sense of community.

6. We reject stigma and do not tolerate discrimination.

- Mental illness carries stigma in society, but within NAMI groups, acceptance and inclusion are key. This principle promotes advocacy, education, and efforts to break down barriers to understanding and acceptance.

7. We won't judge anyone's pain as less than our own.

- Everyone's struggles are valid, and no one's pain is "worse" or "less important" than another's. This fosters an environment of empathy, where individuals feel heard and supported without comparison or competition.

8. We forgive ourselves and reject guilt.

- Mental illness can lead to feelings of guilt or self-blame. This principle encourages self-compassion, reminding individuals that they are not at fault for their illness or past struggles.

9. We embrace humor as healthy.

- Laughter and lightheartedness can be powerful tools for healing. While struggles are real, finding moments of humor can reduce stress and bring a sense of normalcy to difficult situations.

10. We accept we cannot solve all problems.

- Not every issue has a simple solution, and that's okay. The goal is to provide support, not to "fix" everything.

Acknowledging this helps reduce pressure and allows for focus on progress rather than perfection.

11. We expect a better future in a realistic way.

- Hope is crucial, but it must be balanced with realism. Recovery takes time, and setbacks may happen, but with support and perseverance, improvement is possible.

12. We will never give up hope.

- No matter the challenges faced, there is always hope for recovery, stability, and a fulfilling life. Encouraging hope is fundamental to fostering resilience and motivation for continued healing.

Group Guidelines

1. Start and stop on time

- Meetings should begin and end at the scheduled times to respect everyone's time and maintain structure. This ensures that all participants can rely on consistency and predictability, which is particularly important in a mental-health-support setting.

2. Time limit for check-in

- Each participant is typically given a set amount of time to share during the check-in portion of the meeting. This prevents any one person from dominating the discussion and ensures that everyone has an opportunity to speak.

3. Absolute confidentiality

- What is shared in the group must remain private. This encourages openness and trust, allowing participants to speak honestly without fear that their personal experiences will be shared outside the group.

4. Be respectful

- Everyone's experiences and perspectives are valid, and participants should treat each other with kindness and consideration. Respect includes listening without judgment, avoiding offensive language, and acknowledging others' feelings.

5. Be mindful of others; no monopolizing or cross talk

- Participants should be aware of how much time they are speaking and allow others the chance to share.
- *No monopolizing:* One person should not dominate the conversation.
- *No cross talk:* Avoid interrupting, giving unsolicited advice, or engaging in side conversations while someone else is speaking.

6. Let's keep it in the here and now

- The focus should be on present experiences and challenges rather than dwelling too much on the past or hypothetical future situations. This helps participants stay grounded and fosters constructive discussions.

7. Empathize with one another's situation

- Rather than offering advice or trying to "fix" someone's problems, group members should provide support through empathy and understanding. This means validating each other's feelings and experiences rather than minimizing or comparing struggles.

A Community Covenant

I have personally been in support groups that read both the principles of support and group guidelines at the beginning of each group session. When leading a group I like to include a guideline about not offering unsolicited advice. Oftentimes, that is not the role of a support group, as we aren't here to solve one another's problems but to support our peers, listen deeply, and be a companion in this journey of healing. But ultimately, you will know your context and should think through possible outcomes when dealing with difficult content such as trauma.

In considering possible outcomes, you can address possible behaviors that may need an additional guideline for your context. Stating these principles and guidelines at the beginning can also bolster your credibility in moderating a conversation. For example, it can give you the space to

remind folks of a particular guideline if you feel someone
has crossed a line. I tend to approach my role as a facilitator
differently than when I'm simply a participant. Depending
on your skills and comfort with facilitation, it's important to
thoughtfully consider which role you'll take on.

Tip:

This may go without saying, but I will say it anyway. If you are
helping to facilitate a group, you might think about what personal
boundaries exist around your own trauma. For instance, if I am
facilitating a group, I don't share all my darkest traumatic stories.
This is a space for the folks who have elected to join the group,
and as a clergyperson, I need to find healthy spaces to verbally
ventilate that aren't with the population I am serving. Remember,
for these group guidelines your main goal is to foster a space that
is filled with "safe enough others" who can offer support to one
another. In other words, you are holding space for this to happen
organically between participants.

When I lead discussion groups for students, I like to begin
by creating a "community covenant." The word "covenant" is
a theological concept that reflects the biblical understanding
of God's relationship with humanity—a relationship marked
by mutual commitment: God's faithfulness to God's people,
and the responsibilities entrusted to humankind.

We gather and worship around a God who is inherently covenantal. God made a covenant with his people in the earliest scriptures in the Bible. Take Abraham in Genesis 12:1–3 and all that has to happen and change between God and his people to lead to God's covenant with Noah (Gen. 9:8–17). God adjusted and reevaluated the covenantal relationship all throughout salvation history. Later, we see the unique development of a covenant with Moses in the burning bush and the Ten Commandments, and we also have the unique covenantal responsibilities of the prophets to speak God's truth (and expectations) to the nations. Then, we have an expanded covenant for all the nations through Christ.

The concept of a covenant also reminds us that there is mutual responsibility within a covenantal relationship. Just as God expected his people to act and treat others in a particular way, when we make a covenant with one another we have a responsibility to act and treat each other with love, kindness, and grace.

In a similar spirit, a community support group works best when its members *covenant* to contribute to the group's well-being. I like to invite the group to determine which guidelines feel most meaningful to them. This practice invites everyone into the shared responsibility of building and sustaining the covenant together.

I may even offer group guidelines of my own that seem fitting for the group, especially with students. This can be a great tool when starting a new discussion group on a difficult

topic (race, socio-economic status, health disparities, etc.). By
mutually agreeing to a community covenant, it helps to maintain important boundaries and find ways to offer appropriate
care and support. Remember: the task of a sharing circle is
to listen and journey alongside, not to fix or solve a personal
problem. Remaining nonjudgmental is key! A community
covenant also places our relationship with one another into
a sacred and even covenantal context. In a way, we are cove-
nanting with one another to walk together in validating and
supportive ways.

An Example of Community Covenant

There is a beautiful little community in the diocese I serve
that talks a lot about mutual deference over personal preference. Sometimes we don't know what traumas individuals
carry with them into our worship spaces. So a posture of
mutual deference makes room for folks to carry whatever
they have without letting a simple personal preference take
priority.

Mutual deference over personal preference is a powerful
concept, especially in the context of faith communities, where
individuals bring a wide range of experiences, needs, and
traumas into shared spaces, and in some cases, even religious
trauma. At its core, mutual deference is about prioritizing
the well-being and needs of the community over personal
desires. It's an intentional posture of humility, patience, and

compassion, recognizing that what might be a simple preference for one person could be a significant source of pain,
anxiety, or, on the flip side, healing for another.

Mutual deference is particularly important when considering trauma. Trauma often leads people to feel powerless
or unsafe, especially in communal settings. By prioritizing
deference, communities create environments where individuals feel honored, included, and cared for—without being
forced to conform to the dominant culture or expectations.

This approach also reflects the covenantal relationships
I mentioned earlier—the understanding that we are bound
not by personal preference, but by a shared commitment to
love, serve, and uplift one another in Christ. Just as Christ
embodied self-giving love, communities that practice mutual
deference reflect a deeper expression of hospitality and grace.

When communities embrace mutual deference, they
become places of refuge and healing. It fosters a sense
of belonging, where everyone—regardless of their past
experiences—feels safe and valued. It transforms spaces from
being merely functional to being sacred, filled with grace and
understanding.

Prompt: Take a moment to imagine what worship might
look like in your community if we valued mutual deference
over personal preference. What personal preference could
you let go of in order to mutually defer to another in your
community?

Tip:

I recommend having participants decide what group guidelines they feel are most important. Another great guideline is to invite people to share only their own experiences, not someone else's experiences. If the group decides on the group guidelines they are often more willing to abide by these guidelines as they have helped draft these boundaries as you engage in the conversation and storytelling. If a group cannot agree on guidelines, you may want to explore the concept of mutual deference over personal preference in that context.

Recently, I facilitated a group of youth students on the topic of anxiety. Perhaps unsurprisingly, they had a lot to say about their experience of anxiety. At the start of our time together I had the students decide what their covenant would be and what mattered to them. They came up with not talking over each other, not offering advice, and listening to one another. We also talked about the importance of confidentiality, agreeing that whatever was shared in that space would remain private. At the same time, we discussed situations where confidentiality might need to be broken, such as my obligation as a mandated reporter. Your group may want to maintain confidentiality as well. In this case, I reminded participants that the only reason I would break confidentiality is if they were hurting themselves or others or someone were hurting them (this typically applies to adults as well).

In my experience, a support group, small group, or sharing circle can be very effective with young adults and students. They are often very prepared and willing to share their experiences and often have a lot of insight into their own behavior in a way that previous generations never had. I encourage you to enjoy these spaces with young people: you may find that you learn a great deal in leading a discussion group in this way.[4]

I want to leave you with a few ideas that are very practical and can be tailored to fit your context. These ideas came forth based on the WCC document I previously mentioned at the beginning of this chapter.

Practical Ideas for Youth Group
Peer-to-Peer Support

You could begin by facilitating spaces for teens to share their experiences and challenges, with an emphasis on mental-health tools such as mindfulness, while using a spiritual grounding or other rituals from the previous chapters to ground the group in Christian principles.

---

4   I use one of my favorite prayer books to address many situations: *Prayers of Honoring Voice* by Pixie Lighthorse (Soulodge, 2016). She is an Indigenous spiritualist and has an amazing way to put words to diverse experiences and generally speaking, in my experience, young folks find her words healing. However, you can use whatever prayer book is a fit in your context.

I have found that intergenerational groups are well received. An intergenerational listening circle could be a group that gathers youth and older parishioners to exchange stories and support one another, fostering trust and connection. When generations get together to actually listen to one another and make room for a variety of voices I have seen the transformational power at work in our parish. You may even want to partner with local professionals in the faith and mental health space to lead workshops and discussions. This could be a short-term program, series, or retreat focused on equipping youth with practical tools for managing stress and anxiety while integrating their faith.

Another approach to group peer-to-peer discussions could include specialized support groups or affinity groups. This would be a group tailored to a specific need such as grief, identity exploration (including LGBTQ+), or managing anxiety and stress. The key to a successful specialized support group is a strong facilitator. A facilitator should be selected with great care. They should be trauma-informed and able to manage difficult conversations with skill. They need to be a validating presence and someone who does not shame or embarrass younger parishioners. Ultimately, it remains very important that any of these group ideas mentioned above operate within a framework that prioritizes safety, respect, validation, and empowerment for all participants.

Chapter 4

Re-membering
What Trauma Has
Fragmented

In 2020, as the world wracked with grief and anger in the wake of George Floyd's death, I like many found myself revisiting memories I hadn't touched in years. Stories of racial trauma, ones that didn't just belong to me but to entire communities, came to the fore of my consciousness. During this time, I decided to share a story in a sermon, one I told with reverence and humility, a story rooted in a small Hawaiian island where histories of pain and beauty that almost transcend this world live side by side.

It has been years since I visited, but certain images remain vivid. I remember how the wind carried the scent of salt and earth. A singular stoplight blinked dutifully in the main village center—a village so small that it seemed to vanish if you blinked. Back then, I was just a teenager from Kailua, living on the more populated island of Oahu, accompanying my youth group on a journey I didn't yet realize would shape me.

Molokai wasn't like the Oahu I knew. It felt quieter, gentler—almost sacred. To get there, we flew on a tiny plane that bucked and hummed more than I liked. I remember gripping the armrest as the turquoise expanse of the Pacific stretched below us. It was only a forty-five-minute flight, but when we landed, it felt as though we had crossed into another world. The land itself seemed to breathe differently.

The Kalaupapa Trail wasn't just a hike—it felt like a test. The path clung desperately to the cliffs, narrow and uneven. I couldn't help but glance down at the waves and foliage. It was like a slow descent into the magic cupboard of C. S. Lewis's *The Lion, the Witch and the Wardrobe*. But in this version my quads were screaming by each mile, and we still had so far to go. Every switchback felt like a small victory, though I wasn't sure whether to look at the cliffs or keep my eyes on my feet. One step down at a time.

Some locals, we learned, relied on mules to commute to their jobs in the historic Kalaupapa Park, including the lone US postal worker who braved the steep trails six days a week. Our host told us that the remaining patients and residents who lived on the peninsula were guided by a rhythm dictated by the isolation: twice a year, a helicopter delivered two large shipments containing all the necessities they would need until the next drop. The thought of relying on just two deliveries a year made the remoteness of the place feel almost unfathomable.

Our hosts were the Indigenous Hawaiian people of Molokai, who welcomed us with a warmth that softened the edges of our teenage awkwardness. They shared their homes, their stories, and their meals, inviting us to sit at their tables and listen. What they didn't say outright, but what I came to feel in every interaction, was that this land held deep wounds. Wounds not easily seen, but impossible to ignore if you paid attention.

Suffice it to say, Kalaupapa's history is far darker than the landscape's beauty would suggest. It reflects a story of terror that, tragically, is not unique among Indigenous communities. Yet there is something profoundly moving in remembering these narratives, walking the land they once inhabited, and viewing the art created by those who lived there under confinement—now commemorated as a historic national park. It is difficult indeed to reconcile such breathtaking surroundings with the weight of the atrocities.

Kalaupapa's history is not unique. Across the globe, Indigenous communities have faced similar atrocities—forced removals, disease, colonization. But there is something profoundly moving about standing in the place where it happened, about walking the same trails, breathing the same air, and seeing the same horizon. It feels like a kind of remembering, one that reaches beyond the mind and into the body.

The natural geography was used to the colonizer's advantage as the ideal place to jail and imprison nearly 8,000 local Indigenous Hawaiians who were exposed to leprosy (now known as Hansen's disease) by the very same people who were colonizing them already. Indigenous people had no immunities or therapies to treat it, which made it highly contagious.

At the time of publication the government-run history and culture site for Kalaupapa says this:

> The government expected that these patients would move into the houses left behind by the Hawaiians who had lived in the area previously, and the ill would tend crops and sustain themselves. But this belief soon proved to be wrong. It soon became apparent that most patients were too ill or demoralized to be self-sufficient. With no hope or will to live, some patients fell into vice and immorality.[1]

Conditions deteriorated quickly. Families filed complaints about the living conditions, and patients were too sick for doctors to visit. Eventually, in the 1900s, the United States government provided the peninsula with two healthcare facilities and more resources. The population decreased as the laws surrounding isolation relaxed over time. However,

---

1   "A Brief History of Kalaupapa," National Parks Service, last updated December 19, 2022, https://www.nps.gov/kala/learn/historyculture/a-brief-history -of-kalaupapa.htm.

it wasn't until 1946 that a cure for Hansen's disease was introduced.

Here is what the history and culture site has to say about the location today:

> Kalaupapa has been home for 100 years for people once banished from society, but it is in transition due to its ever-decreasing patient population. The settlement is much quieter than it once was. There are fewer buildings. Life today is lived at a somewhat slower pace. But Kalaupapa remains a remarkable place with an extraordinary history—a place exhibiting the worst and the best of human responses to the challenge of sickness.[2]

One can imagine the generational trauma of having an ill parent or grandparent ripped from your family home and isolated to a region that is unreachable, without advanced technology to communicate, check in, or visit.

Today, most of the patients have since died. Once cured, some patients elected to stay on the peninsula, which had become their new home. As these patients are dying, it becomes a serious imperative to remember the pain of this history, particularly through oral history. Remembering is an important part of facing our trauma. And remembering is not for the faint of heart. It takes great bravery to remember and to tell the difficult stories of our ancestors. But the only

---

2 National Parks Service, "Kalaupapa."

way to grow as a people and to grow as a community is to tell and retell these histories.

Remembering generational trauma is intrinsically part of the Christian story. The Psalms remember both the triumphs of the Lord and also the struggle and pain of God's people, including their time as slaves in Egypt and captives in Babylon. The act of remembering opens us up to the possibility of God's healing, to the possibility of God's grace. Without remembering first, one can miss the ways that God's grace indeed speaks to our soul wounds. I'm not advocating for a quick turn from pain to healing. Oftentimes, this process of remembering isn't linear and can take decades to unpack.

No matter what type of psychic or physical wounds you carry from trauma, remembering is complicated. It's complicated by patchy memories, differing memories from other family members, and the very fallen and thus humanness of memory. I'm sure you know the experience of retelling a simple story, and your partner, spouse, or best friend remembers the same story entirely differently than you. We know the imperfection of memory, but that doesn't have to keep us from trying. Remembering is a precursor to *re-membering*, that is, rebuilding disparate "members" of your traumatized heart and spirit. In this sense, memory helps the processes of *"re-membering"* what trauma has fragmented, allowing the fractured self (and community) to be knit together again in love. It begins to re-member the fragmented bits of community that may have been lost otherwise.

Re-membering is for the whole Body of Christ, but it is also for your own individual soul. Re-membering your own spirit that may have felt torn apart by a traumatic situation.

Remembering and recounting stories of historical trauma—like that of the Indigenous Hawaiian community forced into isolation at Kalaupapa—is essential for healing. Within a trauma-informed space, such remembrance is not a passive recollection but an intentional act that acknowledges past suffering, honors those who endured it, and helps to *re-member* fragmented lives and communities. By confronting painful histories rather than dismissing or sanitizing them, we open ourselves to the possibility of divine grace, the restoration of wholeness, and the healing presence of God that transforms memory into a source of communal and spiritual resilience.

Reimagine Re-Membering

The history of the Indigenous Hawaiian community at Kalaupapa offers a poignant illustration of how racial and generational trauma can run very deep. Decades of forced isolation, brought on by colonizers who introduced diseases and dismantled longstanding cultural traditions, inflicted immense suffering that rippled through families and communities.

We know that many other Indigenous peoples have experienced similar horrors. Many of whose lands, bodies, and histories were systematically violated. The story of Kalaupapa is an example of how wounds didn't just impact individual lifetimes but spanned generations. Its effects rippled out to impact future generations as well. These wounds, rooted in colonial intrusion and racialized policies, had to be shared, told, and passed down. We carry our ancestors' pain whether we like it or not.

But what can we do with that pain? I contend, as I have earlier in this book, we must become cycle breakers. It is up to us to break the cycles of abuse, dehumanization, and oppression that run through our families, that define our own generational traumas. We have the choice now, today, to make a different path forward. It may take a lot of hard work and some struggle, but with the right people around you and the right type of support and community, you can get there.

As the beloved community—called to be Christ's hands and feet in a wounded world—we must take intentional steps toward breaking cycles of generational trauma. My prayer is that you will commit to educating yourself about any painful legacies you might be attached to albeit oppressor or oppressed. If you don't know your history you are bound to repeat it. This must be a commitment beyond simple awareness; we must embrace the spiritual practice of listening deeply. I believe that God wants to *re-member* each of us. But we have to help ourselves along the way; this is an earned healing. And not the type of earning that a straight-A student does. No, it's the type of healing that comes with inner peace, a peace that knows what has been broken and leads us all closer to reconciliation and restored wholeness.

One way to cope with our lingering burdens is through journaling and other forms of verbal processing. I know that this ritual has helped me, and I have begun to move toward deeper self-understanding and closer communion with the God who created me. And not despite my trauma but because of it. It's for this reason that I believe it may be helpful for you as well. Even if you're not accustomed to journaling, I encourage you to experiment with this practice—try it for just two weeks and observe what unfolds within you.

The exercise I recommend comes from Julia Cameron's *The Artist's Way*, specifically her "Morning Pages" practice. Each morning, as soon as you wake, write three pages without prompts or an agenda—simply let the words flow. When I first tried this, I discovered that my heart felt unblocked, as though I had released a weight I wasn't even aware of. You can always stop if you find it unhelpful, but you might be surprised at what emerges. This approach aligns with the "verbal ventilation" discussed in chapter 3, a concept Pete Walker advocates for in his work on complex PTSD. My suggestion brings together both ways: Pete Walker's psychological insights along with Julia Cameron's creative approach.

In my own experience, these morning pages often begin with basic observations: the clutter on my desk, the dim predawn light, and the faint stirrings of the world outside. Over time, I find myself turning inward, noting subtle shifts in my mood or sensations in my body. Naming these internal landscapes on paper clears my mind and unblocks my spirit. While Cameron's method was developed for artistic pursuits, I have found it to be a nourishing part of my daily prayer. Sometimes, the energy from parishioners feels overwhelming. Sometimes, there are so many thoughts, ideas, and histories to sift through I find that I need time to clear my mind; thus, my spirit feels lighter, leaving me free to engage in my daily responsibilities with greater ease, focus, and grace.

Tip:

If you are a clergyperson who carries significant trauma, I recommend this exercise of morning pages to you. I think you may find it soothing and helpful to write your story down, even if you never share it with anyone but God.

Adverse Childhood Experiences

Remembering is also difficult because there are times when we simply do not want to put the work and effort into remembering. Childhood trauma can often function this way. I want to make some recommendations for those who have experienced adverse childhood experiences (ACEs).

First, if you are uncertain about your childhood or you don't know where to start, I'd encourage you to look at the CDC website on the topic.[3] On the adverse-childhood-experiences site you can find an ACEs quiz, which will give you an idea about where your childhood falls on a scale that meets today's standards. I recently took the quiz, and I have an ACE score of 7 out of 10, with 10 being the highest level of trauma. You are not alone! I'd encourage you to use this as a starting point for journaling and therapy. I also think it will help you understand and digest this chapter. So take a moment to head over there, take your ACEs quiz, and see where you fall.

I want to leave you with one more invaluable theory called the internal-family-systems model, and the preeminent book on the topic is Richard Schwartz's work entitled *No Bad Parts*. His work pushes back on the "mono-mind perspective," that is, "the idea that you have one mind, out of which different thoughts and emotions and impulses and urges emanate."[4] This may sound quite reasonable, as many of us simply accept this view. However, Schwartz lays out a different paradigm. He articulates how we are complex humans with histories, stories that shape us, and there are facets to each of our personalities, and these complexities are

---

3   "Adverse Childhood Experiences," Centers for Disease Control, accessed March 25, 2025, https://www.cdc.gov/aces/about/index.html.
4   Schwartz, *No Bad Parts*, 7.

more accurately reflected in a vision such as "internal family systems." Some of those internal parts happen to sound a lot like our mother, father, siblings. Moreover, some of those internal parts are helpful and others are harmful.

I'll give you a personal example: much of my inner voice is critical and reflects the way my own mother spoke to me. It's taken intentional work and deep reflection to evaluate that inner voice and to learn to say "no" to it when it's no longer serving me.

Schwartz's work uses helpful reflective exercises to unwind some of what one might carry along with them from childhood experiences and the internal voices that developed there in, particularly if those experiences were adverse childhood experiences.

Tip:

Schwartz's book is an excellent resource to have on hand to offer folks who might be struggling with adverse childhood experiences, particularly given a rise of estranged parent-child relationships within our already fragmented country. In 2024, the *New Yorker* came out with an article entitled "Why So Many People Are Going 'No Contact' With Their Parents."[5] I predict that the continued rise of polarization within our nation will inevitably continue this trend.

---

5   Anna Russell, "Why So Many People Are Going 'No Contact' with Their Parents," *New Yorker*, August 30, 2024, https://www.newyorker.com/culture/annals-of-inquiry/why-so-many-people-are-going-no-contact-with-their-parents.

For those readers who carry deep psychic wounds from childhood, I want to reiterate that you are not alone. Even when it feels like no one else in the world understands your position, this work, this very book, is for the ones who don't go back for family holidays because of what happened to them. This is for the ones who have carried their pain all alone, who suffer in silence and may even be too afraid to face the truth. It is for the ones who are just coming to terms with their adverse childhood experiences. Healing work may feel like a struggle, but in reality, it is growth. And growth often requires something of us—patience, endurance, and trust in the unseen work happening beneath the surface.

Consider the mustard seed, the very first of its kind, spoken into existence by the God of the universe. Tiny and buried deep within the earth, it seems hidden, insignificant. Yet within its small shell, transformation is taking place. Nourished by water and sunlight, the seed breaks open, releasing a fragile sprout that pushes upward, reaching for the light.

It struggles through the dirt, pressing past resistance, until one day, it emerges above the surface. What this tiny sprout does not yet know is that it will grow into a tree of immense strength—a towering refuge that offers shade and shelter to the land's inhabitants.

And so it is with you. Growth may feel like struggle, but something powerful is happening beneath the surface. Keep reaching. Keep growing. One day, you will see just how strong you have become.

Be brave.

Now, while you may not discuss the deepest aspects of your childhood hurt in a corporate or public setting—perhaps finding healing through journaling or with a professional therapist—I do believe there is a collective traumatic experience we can all relate to and that we might benefit from hearing each other's stories about: the pandemic of 2020.

As mentioned before, one small way to foster healing in a religious setting is by creating a community support group focused on discussing the effects of the global pandemic. This is a shared social experience of recent memory—what I consider "low-hanging fruit"—because we all went through it in some form. Each of us has felt its impact in deeply personal ways: some lost family members, others lost longtime parishioners, and still others experienced disproportionate hardships due to their roles as frontline workers or the marginalization of their identities. The questions that follow are ones I've asked myself and believe could open meaningful dialogue in a parish group setting.

I've even begun using some of these questions in pastoral care settings. These are questions I would genuinely love to ask every parishioner and try to hear and understand their experiences and points of view.

1. What was difficult spiritually, emotionally, and physically about the global pandemic?
2. What fears, losses, or anxieties did you experience? What did you do to grieve or lament these?
3. How did our corporate behavior during the pandemic help or hinder your ability to find community?
4. Did you witness the experiences of frontline workers or marginalized communities? How did/does this impact your understanding of injustice, empathy, and community?
5. How did the pandemic change or challenge your faith and theological understanding?

To remember one's history is not easy. It requires more than just reading or listening. It demands that we sit with the discomfort, that we confront the pain, and that we carry these stories forward. Remembering is an act of bravery, but it is also an act of love—for the people who endured, for the land that holds their memory, and for the future we hope to build.

As we hiked back up the trail, the sun was beginning to set, casting long shadows over the cliffs. The switchbacks seemed steeper on the way up, and my legs ached with every step. But there was something sacred in the climb, something that felt like honoring those who had walked this path before us. I didn't have the words for it then, but I understand now:

to remember is to bear witness. And to bear witness is to keep the stories alive.

Molokai taught me that memory is a kind of resistance. It is a way of saying, *we will not forget*. And in a world that so often tries to erase, there is so much power in that.

Chapter 5

Sacred Spaces and Safety

Introduction: What Makes a Space Sacred?

In the heart of the Boston area, a gothic-style building harbors the Society of Saint John the Evangelist, an Episcopal monastic order. It was the first stable religious community for a group of monastic men in the Anglican Church since the Reformation.[1] The brothers now live admirably under a detailed rule of life, and at their profession of faith, they make vows of poverty, celibacy, and obedience.[2] Monastic orders are not unfamiliar in the Episcopal Church and many other churches. But what made my visit so meaningful was how the brothers spoke about the intentionality of the space.

I visited for the first time in 2024, and as soon as I entered the sanctuary, the space seemed to shift. The light streamed in from small windows near the ceiling. Sitting to observe the

---

1   "SSJE: Our History," Society of Saint John the Evangelist, accessed March 26, 2025, https://www.ssje.org/our-history/.

2   SSJE, "Our History."

architecture, the shift in light and the scent of wax burning on the Christ candle near the altar warmed my spirit. Even the cold grey bricks were warm and inviting. After spending time in their sanctuary, we were escorted down a narrow hallway into the bowels of the building where a community room that resembled a casual dining area, perhaps used for the brothers to eat breakfast, was located.

In the middle stood a large kitchen-style table surrounded by plenty of seating. We spoke with one of the brothers for a while, and he was welcoming and answered our many questions. Throughout our conversation, it became clear how thoughtful the brothers were in their use of space. Their rule of life included the sacredness of their space. The sanctuary, divided into two main areas, looks like an ancient basilica. One area features traditional pews facing forward, much like a typical church. In contrast, the second area—the space where the brothers regularly worship—had chairs arranged in two rows facing each other along the left and right sides of the room. At the center of the room was a large baptismal font, which seemed to anchor the room just as much as it anchored our hearts.

As the light trickled in on the grey day of our visit, the brother who guided us explained to our group that facing one another during the liturgy reminds them of the deep community they participate in. They can easily see each other, make eye contact, and feel united. The worship experience is about what we see, learn, and appreciate in one another as fellow travelers in this life together.

Ultimately, this sacred space told us a story. It told us a story about its history in the ancient basilica-style architecture. It told us a story about its sacramental nature through the Christ candle, the altar, and the font. And to my mind, most importantly, it told us a story about the community. Sacred space tells a story. What story do you want your sacred space to tell?

In this chapter, I have divided my considerations into two categories: in-person sacred space and online sacred space. For part 1, I will consider four areas: physical safety, emotional safety, cultural safety, and relational safety. While I don't think online spaces can or should replace our in-person sacred space, we can't ignore that creating holy space online is foundational for the future of the Christian church in our modern world. These online spaces will be the topic of part two of this chapter.

Physical Safety

Physical safety is the most concrete and obvious. Reshaping sacred space can mean letting in natural light, using fewer hierarchies, or rethinking what "reverence" looks like. I know of a worship setting where the sermon rotates among individuals each week. It is often delivered as a story without a pulpit, with time for the congregation to share personal reflections.

This is such a brilliant and creative way to invert hierarchies and foster a safer space for those who have experienced spiritual trauma or similar abuses.

Some of the more prominent examples that make a variety of individuals feel safe and secure may include accessibility, emergency preparedness, and child and vulnerable adult safety. It may mean creating a dedicated area in the adult sanctuary that is incredibly safe and welcoming for children, with age-appropriate toys and activities to engage them during worship. It might mean providing audio devices for those with hearing difficulties. It could also be as simple as offering a warm and welcoming greeting to everyone who walks through the door. The possibilities, indeed, are endless.

Here are some questions you might explore with your congregation and within your setting:

1. What story does our current space tell?
2. What story do we want our sacred space to tell?
3. After you know the story you want to tell, think through *how* to put that story within the space. What items can you use? What changes will you make? What improvements do you want to make? Use various creative and resourceful ideas to accomplish the story you want to tell.
4. Be sure to consider varied learning styles, liturgical styles, and cultures.

Emotional Safety

For some, the act of Communion—a ritual meant to unite us with Christ's body and blood—can instead evoke pain or confusion. Serene Jones, in her book *Trauma and Grace*, recounts the story of a parishioner who experienced a traumatic response during Communion, fleeing to the bathroom, overcome with guilt and disorientation. What was intended to be a sacred space of comfort in Christ had suddenly become a place of fear and disconnection. Even a holy space can feel unsafe for those carrying past wounds.

Church buildings, rituals, and relationships alike can come with the weight of spiritual trauma, whether it be purity culture, exclusionary or exploitative practices, or other forms of past abuse. With careful attention to emotional safety, we may have the chance to reduce barriers to entry and make entering these spaces feel less overwhelming.

We can begin by meeting people where they are—whether at Bible study, noon-day prayer, Compline, or small groups. One tool that can be effective is a spiritual grounding. Much like a sailor uses a drift marker off in the distance to anchor his direction, a spiritual grounding offers participants a sense of calm and connection in moments that might otherwise be overwhelming.

I recently spoke to a person with severe religious trauma. They had experienced challenges around queer identity within a very different tradition, a tradition that wasn't forthcoming about their beliefs but lured crowds in with catchy music and hipster pastors. This person shared with me that during their time at this regressive church they began to experience thoughts of self-harm and even suicide. They openly shared that this church community glossed over such serious concerns with "thoughts and prayers"—a classic phrase that in many ways has become almost meaningless as it is used far too often in preventable and tragic incidents. Even if the intention is good, the phrase has almost lost its meaning. This church also made mental health claims that were, simply put, harsh and unhelpful. This story is far too common in certain church settings.

At this junction my friend reached out to a Unitarian Universalist pastor, and while this is not the tradition I currently come from, I think we can learn a lot from this pastor's compassion. When the pastor became alerted to this parishioner's suicidal thoughts, she said: "Pack a bag of things you will need for a week or so; I will come pick you up and we will go to an intake appointment together."

It is clear from the story that this UU pastor had direct experience coming alongside others who may be faced with mental illness. It didn't appear to be an unfamiliar scenario for her. She seemed to walk through this exchange with experience and grace.

This pastor's response to a parishioner's anguish stands out to me. Instead of defaulting to emergency intervention, she provided direct support, ensuring the individual received medical attention in a compassionate and controlled manner. She continued to visit, write letters of encouragement, and walk alongside this person throughout their healing journey and recovery. Though the individual still carries wounds from past religious experiences, hope and healing now coexist.

With the rise of mental health conditions affecting our communities, it is more crucial than ever for clergy to understand how to guide individuals toward proper care. Stories like this remind me that there are still pastors and priests committed to walking alongside those in crisis, offering not just faith but tangible support. And that gives me hope.

Spiritual Grounding as a Form of Healing

I want to leave you with a very practical tool that can be used in a variety of situations. When one's mental health is in crisis, a Spiriutal Grounding may be a helpful tool. Below I have shared a script I wrote for my own spiritual grounding. You can either adapt it to fit your theological context or use it as written. This practice can set the tone for emotional safety or create a foundation of trust for group discussions. It can be used individually or in a group setting.

Spiritual Grounding Script:

Welcome to our discussion today. I am so grateful you have chosen to be here. Let us begin with grounding ourselves. This practice sets out to help us settle into ourselves while remembering that God is Emmanuel, God with us. I encourage you to place your feet flat on the floor remembering that the earth that God created is beneath your feet and connects us all to one another. If you are sitting in a chair, try to find a comfortable position, preferably allowing your feet to press into the floor beneath you. You may notice aches and pains as you move through this exercise; that's normal, and it's okay! Take a deep breath through your nose and into your chest, let it fill your belly, hold it in for one or two seconds, and then release it softly and slowly: belly, chest, throat, and mouth. Let's try the same thing again. (Pause for a deep breath.) Let each breath remind you of God's spirit.

Now, I invite you to draw your attention to your head. Remember that God is always above you, and you are never alone. Soften the muscles around your face and neck, and breathe into any tension you may be noticing. (Pause) Now, breathe awareness into your upper shoulders and down your back. You might sit up tall and straighten your spine. Now, bring your attention to your arms and hands. Maybe relax your fingers and wiggle them a bit. You might consider placing your hands face up on your lap as a posture showing you are ready to receive what God has for you today. Now, draw your attention to your legs and feet. Feel your body resting upon the chair. (Pause)

Take another deep breath as before. (Pause) When you are ready, slowly open your eyes and wiggle your toes and fingers to bring yourself back into your body. Amen.

After leading a spiritual grounding, consider offering a space for reflection. Invite participants to share what they felt within their bodies. What did they find helpful, and what did they find challenging? All thoughts and feelings about this exercise are welcome. Some folks might resist this practice, and that's okay. Emotional safety is a journey; it may take time to realize how much one's body needs regular spiritual grounding. The ending of a spiritual grounding is crucial; I'd recommend that you plan to transition gently into group discussions or activities to maintain a calm and reflective atmosphere.

As I mentioned, a spiritual grounding is not just for group settings. Parishioners can also do a spiritual grounding individually at home. Lay leaders can lead them. The uses are open ended. Offering this tool to parishioners to use at home can empower them on their healing journey. Spiritual grounding provides a way forward for many types of trauma, and a priest isn't required for this practice; anyone can do it.

Tip:

One important note is that when I lead a spiritual grounding like this, the ending is crucial. You need time to transition between this more profound bodily practice and a conversation, such as in a support group or Bible study. A spiritual grounding needs to land smoothly, like an airplane's landing. If you decide not to use my script, consider how you want to invite folks to "reawaken" their bodies after this soothing experience.

Below are some follow-up questions that you can ask folks to allow time to reflect on this exercise in a group or individual setting. I especially like leading discussions with these follow-up questions because sometimes folks can learn from one another:

- How was that experience for you?
- Did you notice something new you hadn't noticed before?
- What was the most challenging part of this grounding meditation?
- Did you sense that God might be communicating a theme, word, or phrase to you?

One thing I've learned over many years of meditative forms of prayer is that one's breath can be a centering feature for any exercise like this. In reality one could use any form of prayer coupled with breath. I've experienced the use of a prayer labyrinth, walking slowly enough to inhale deeply over one or two steps, and releasing that deep breath slowly, again and again. Being guided by the pathway ahead and completely caught up in the present moment of prayer. But there are physical benefits too, not just spiritual or mental ones.

This type of breathwork can help regulate your nervous system and prayer is so much more than a mental or intellectual enterprise. When we incorporate breathing, or moving (as in a prayer labyrinth), our prayer in fact becomes embodied! Embodied meaning our whole selves are involved.

I took a very formative Anglican studies class and one of the priests taught me so much about how we can pray our Episcopal prayers using our breath. Many parishes use a practice called "pointing" to indicate certain notation for the organist and singers, and some communities also use the symbol of an asterisk to indicate particular details about the recitation. Such as when the whole congregation responds, for instance. But in this small Anglican formation setting we used the asterisk at the end of each line of the psalms as a reminder to take a deep inhale and to let your long full breath exhale on the next line. It wasn't until I experienced this practice of deep breathing while we prayed together in community that I found a new sense of peace even from the old familiar words.

Cultural and Relational Safety

Spiritual grounding can offer a sense of calm and centered-ness. Its primary goal is internal, helping individuals find stability within themselves. However, cultural and relational safety extends beyond the individual—it focuses on how we relate to one another within community. It is about creating environments where everyone feels seen, valued, and respected, especially those from historically marginalized or underrepresented groups.

Let me offer a practical example. I was at a parish that hosted an affinity event designed to create a safe space for LGBTQ+ members of the community. That afternoon, folding tables were covered with fabric, and mismatched yarn kept rolling off the edges. The event was billed as a social night for introverts, centered around handcrafts. Sticks from parishioners' yards were collected for making God's-eye crafts, and guests were invited to bring any personal projects they were working on.

While the crafts set a gentle, welcoming tone, the real highlight of the evening came from an unexpected collaborative art project. Even if you don't have access to an art therapist, there are many ways to create community art where expression, creativity, and culture can shine.

When the therapist brought out paint markers and brushes, some participants hesitated—many hadn't done anything like this since childhood. But soon, buttons, paper cups, feathers, pipe cleaners, and vibrant colors spilled across the canvas. It was clearly the work of many hands—alive, joyful, and wholly unique. Today, it hangs in our parish hall, surrounded by handwritten acknowledgments and apologies from the artists. It doesn't just hang there—it breathes.

At the end of the evening, a parishioner approached me and said, "I've never been in a church where I didn't feel like a stranger—until now. Tonight, I felt at home. Thank you." My heart soared to know that even one person felt more at home in our sacred space.

It was as if the feathers and fabric they had added to the collage shimmered—bright, unapologetic. Beneath the artwork, the words of acknowledgment and apology served as a living witness: This is what safety looks like when people are allowed to bring their full selves into the room.

So, how can a community begin to offer these spaces of radical welcome?

First, we must acknowledge and address historical harms. The Episcopal Church has a history entangled with colonialism. Some members carry personal experiences of being unwelcome or unaccepted by faith communities. Many dioceses and congregations have begun the important work of making reparations to Indigenous communities on whose land our churches are built. Our denomination also wrestles with its silence during the enslavement of African peoples. Acknowledging these historic harms is vital to making sacred spaces safer. Ignoring these truths can perpetuate harm, especially for those from historically oppressed communities. By openly acknowledging institutional wounds, we can begin to ask for forgiveness and rebuild trust.

Second, we must cultivate leadership that reflects the diversity of the wider community—across age, gender, race, and socioeconomic background. One of the greatest joys of that art night was watching people of all ages co-create a vibrant work together. Diverse leadership signals to people that their voices matter. To avoid tokenizing individuals, diversity must be reflected at every level of decision-making.

Empower leaders to be substantive partners, not symbolic ones. And when working in diverse teams, invest in anti-racism, implicit bias, and cultural competency training to strengthen the bonds of trust and understanding.

Finally, honor people's whole identities. Affirm and celebrate them fully—race, culture, gender, orientation, and beyond. People should feel free to bring their whole selves into sacred spaces. Use inclusive language in worship. Acknowledge cultural holidays like Juneteenth and Indigenous Peoples' Day. Make it clear, in word and in deed, that their stories and traditions are welcome and cherished.

Above all, radical welcome is about valuing each voice equally—in vestry conversations, in worship, and in all aspects of communal life. When everyone's voice matters, true belonging becomes possible.

Sacred Spaces in the Digital Age

Digital spaces are an extension of our in-person sacred spaces, and we need to approach them with the same intention-ality and care. Just as in-person holy space is an extension of our mission, so is the space we create digitally. You might consider asking yourself and your parish leaders if your church's mission is communicated through the online worship spaces you create. The same concepts of emotional, physical, cultural, and relational safety that apply to in-person sacred spaces also apply to digital spaces.

I have personally led and been a member of a number of online healing groups, some with the theme of trauma, some with the theme of mutual support. Some have more explicit ties to holistic ways of healing. I have personally found that online support groups have allowed me to connect with individuals who I may not have ordinarily connected with.

However, my interest in online forms of ministry really took root during the pandemic when nearly all small churches had to move their ministries entirely online. Seminary hadn't exactly prepared me for the digital age of ministry, but being a millennial helped. At the time, I was working part-time in a parish and was a key player in helping to bring our worship online, learning new platforms, and streamlining our work and communication within the parish. Like many churches, we experimented with prerecorded services, hybrid services, and live streams.

I remember trying to process this massive shift in our ministry formulation. As a fresh seminary graduate, I had never considered that every sermon might be videotaped and saved on a YouTube channel indefinitely. At first, the idea of being able to examine mistakes, miscommunications, and liturgy indefinitely was daunting. However, I've now come to enjoy online ministry, partly because I've seen how it can connect like-minded individuals near and far!

First, it will be critical to consider how online spaces impact those we serve. Would your view of online ministry change if I told you that most sources say that many

Americans spend two to three hours daily on social media? The second part of my question is: do parishioners see you as a clergyperson or church leader in those spaces? Part of the impetus for online ministry is understanding that we need progressive church leaders and their voices to be found within these online spaces.

Just as with in-person sacred spaces, online sacred spaces must seek to meet people where they are. During COVID-19, our parish experimented with the live premiere feature on YouTube. Our new form of worship allowed us as clergy to be moderators in the chat during the service since it was a prerecorded service, and we were all still worshipping at home. While it is not practical for clergy to take on this role on regular Sunday mornings, I saw the possibility for a virtual "usher" to moderate the live chat for those watching worship online.

A live chat can create conversations between homebound parishioners in a way that was not possible previously. While we can't precisely communicate the bread and wine through the internet, we can build friendships and create an emotionally safe space for people to come to online worship just as they are. I see relational connections as a way to extend the gift of our sacraments through these electronic means. Of course, this doesn't replace the critical role of lay eucharistic ministers who visit those who cannot attend church to receive Communion. But opening up the live chat for conversation can be welcoming to many folks who find community in this way.

The main point of sharing this story is that I hope you will consider the possibilities of technology that, when considered ethically and intentionally, can be utilized as a tool to create deeper community. Building community through technology can help us maintain our connections in profound ways. Below I have given you some examples for those who stream live on YouTube. One first step could include opening up your live chat feature. If this is a type of community you are interested in developing for your parishioners here are some suggestions if you decide you want to open your live stream chat feature:

- Use parish volunteers to moderate the chat. Moderators can protect the chat from disruptive comments, such as those made by online trolls.
- Ask an usher or young adult to help be a moderator. Perhaps ask someone planning to be on their computer for worship so as not to pull folks away from their in-person worship.
- Get a good rotation of moderators so it doesn't fall on just one person.
- Ask young adults if they are willing to help build a team of moderators.

I regularly join live-chat streams to see what it's like, and I can attest to the sense of community that builds when you watch a live stream with other people's comments. You can chat back and forth with different folks, see how other people are responding, and learn a lot about what you are watching and how it is being received.

I've observed that a chat feature can be incredibly impactful for those missing their in-person community and the friendships built over time within a parish setting, mainly the homebound. This feature has the possibility of connecting survivors of trauma, even survivors of a particular type of trauma, who may not have been able to communicate in previous generations due to travel requirements or sheer distance between individuals. Now, someone from California can find someone from Ohio who has had a similar traumatic experience and realize how un-alone they are.

Sacred spaces, whether digital or in-person, tell a story. They reflect and communicate the values of a particular religious community. With intentionality, we can seek and begin to convey the right message of inclusivity, God's abiding love for all, and our ongoing advocacy for those who are most vulnerable among us. So, what story does your sacred space tell? And what story do you want it to tell?

PART 2

Introduction to Part 2

$\mathcal{T}$he following chapters are a brief primer on three types of traumatic experiences: domestic violence, spiritual/religious abuse, and racial trauma. Our baptismal covenant asks us to uphold the dignity of all people, which includes those who carry trauma. My intention for this primer is to familiarize you with these types of trauma and some of the challenges and nuances that exist in these conversations. Before diving into these specific trauma categories, I want to root our conversation in urgent realities facing young people today. This information can function to help us honor the dignity of all people and widen our understanding of the scope of human experiences.

In 2024 the World Council of Churches came out with a message entitled "A Call for Cross-Generational Action on the Mental Health of Youth." This message, born from a joint working group on mental health by the Commission of the Churches on Health and Healing, clearly sets forth that call to action:

> Given the limited access to Mental Health Care and professionals,
> it is vital that Faith Communities, which are present all over

the world and have networks and support systems in place, be mobilized to promote Mental Health of youth in an informed, safe, supportive, sustainable manner, in close collaboration with Mental health professionals.[1]

When I see statistics from the CDC—like in 2021 "more than 4 in 10 (42 percent) students felt persistently sad or hopeless and nearly one-third (29 percent) experienced poor mental health" and "more than 1 in 5 (22 percent) students seriously considered attempting suicide and 1 in 10 (10 percent) attempted suicide"—I was dumbfounded by the numbers. I asked myself, how am I not talking about youth mental health every single day in our ministry, knowing that at least some of our students must have experienced this? A mental health crisis can be commonplace for many families, and we must find ways to address this with our fellow siblings. My pastoral concerns are compounded when we think about other identities that are at a higher risk:

- "These feelings of distress were found to be more common among LGBTQ+ students, female students, and students across racial and ethnic groups.

---

1   World Council of Churches, Joint Working Group, "A Call for Cross-Generational Action on the Mental Health of Youth," August 12, 2024, https://www.oikoumene.org/sites/default/files/2024-08/WCC-%20A%20call%20for%20cross-generational%20action%20on%20the%20Mental%20Health%20of%20Youth.pdf.

- Nearly half (45 percent) of LGBQ+ students in 2021 seriously considered attempting suicide—far more than heterosexual students.
- Black students were more likely to attempt suicide than students of other races and ethnicities."[2]

If you're a young person reading this: Hi, my friend. I hope the tools and stories I've shared so far help you feel even a little less alone. So many others are living with that same heaviness—anxiety, dread, and deep sadness. I've been there too. I've had nights where the tears wouldn't stop. I've had moments when everything hurt so much that I didn't want to be here anymore. That pain can feel like a weight in your chest, spreading through your whole body.

If you're feeling that way now, please know that the most important thing you can do is reach out. You don't have to keep reading—take a moment, pause here, and talk to someone you trust. You deserve support.

Try to find a trusted adult—someone who you know will treat you with care and not cause harm. Tell them what you're going through. It might not be your parents, and that's okay. Maybe it's a school counselor, a teacher, a coach, or someone else you trust. Be creative.

---

2 "Adolescent and School Health," Centers for Disease Control, accessed March 26, 2025, https://www.cdc.gov/healthy-youth/.

You are not meant to carry this alone. No one is. Please—
reach out and ask for help. You are worthy of support, and
you are not alone in this.

I'm not here to promise you that every priest and every
pastor is going to know how to respond to this weight you
are carrying. I pray you have someone in your faith community that you can trust. And I want you to know that we are
beginning to talk about it—*it* being mental health! We (the
older generations) are trying to face it in ourselves so we can
learn and walk alongside you in authentic ways. We are trying
to become a better community that can foster resilience and
emotional and mental health. We are striving to create spaces
that promote healthy relationships and deep community in
order to bring about these efforts.

If you're someone older—perhaps an older Millennial,
part of Gen X, or a Boomer: Hi there! I'm so grateful you're
taking the time to learn more about the realities of trauma
in our parishes and in the lives of young people today. These
conversations can be tender and challenging, but please don't
let that hold you back. Your care and willingness to engage
can help create systems of real support.

The World Council of Churches offers fourteen practical suggestions for how faith communities can become
safer, more informed spaces that support mental health and
respond to trauma. I encourage you to read them, reflect
on them, and consider how they might come to life in your
own parish setting. And most importantly, take to heart

their call to "strengthen cross-generational communication and . . . accompany youth to deepen faith in God and strengthen engagement within faith communities."

There are a number of types of trauma that distinctly increase vulnerability of our youth. These effects include:

1) Violence and conflict: The message from the WCC says, "Even in regions free of open conflicts and wars, children and youth who face a micro-climate of normalized violence . . . are highly vulnerable."

2) Systemic challenges in society: The message from the WCC says, "Inequities in societies with regard to access to services, facilities, opportunities for education technology and work are contributing to a paucity of hope and the dimming of perceived future prospects."

3) Ignorance, stigma, and exclusion: The message from the WCC says: "The lack of awareness of mental health in many societies, the reluctance to discuss issues openly and the stigma associated with mental health conditions make youth who are already vulnerable even more vulnerable."

These are all reasons why in part 2 I provide a primer on three types of trauma. These primers are not designed to give you the ability to "diagnose" or to even offer a definitive "prognosis." These primers are simply to give you a window into some of the details of a particular type of trauma and to offer suggestions for remaining a supportive community member and clergyperson.

Chapter 6

Domestic Violence Primer

Introduction: A Theological Framework

How long, O Lord? How long will the cries of those trapped in violence go unheard? How long will silence and shame keep them isolated? How long will it be before someone makes their safety known to them?

Jesus's cry to God while hanging upon the cross is relatable for those who suffer from domestic abuse. In his hour of great need and near his death, Jesus utters a cry to God that is reminiscent of the twenty-second Psalm: "My God, my God, why have you forsaken me? Why are you so far from helping me, from the words of my groaning?" (Ps. 22:1–2 NRSV)

Domestic violence is a particular type of trauma that runs deep. It happens in many relationships and touches on several power dynamics and imbalances. These dynamics are complex and often bump up against each other, requiring continuous learning and understanding. I will expound on power dynamics later in this chapter and offer a tool to evaluate some of the power dynamics in a given situation. This chapter is merely to provide a window into the complexities of domestic violence because understanding the nuance and challenges can help us care for those within our spiritual care.

As clergy, our role is not to diagnose but to provide support and understanding. This chapter is designed to bring greater understanding and a more profound sensitivity to domestic violence, a reality that may exist in our parishes. It is crucial and responsible for me to restate that clergy are not social workers, therapists, or medical doctors. We must remain diligent when referring parishioners out to various professionals whenever it is necessary. Always ensure you understand the expectations of reporting, particularly, if you are a mandated reporter! More on this later in the chapter that comes ahead.

Understanding Domestic Violence:
Definitions and Scope

Domestic violence affects all races, socioeconomic levels, generations, and various identities. There is so much stigma with domestic violence that often it is kept a secret. So, the belief that it doesn't exist in your parish or perhaps your circle of influence is unlikely. Domestic violence affects all genders. In some cases, a person may be surprised to learn that even men can be violated in a domestic-violence situation by female partners. According to the CDC, one in three men experience sexual violence, physical violence, or stalking by an intimate partner within their lifetime.[1] (Incidentally, I am not aware of nationwide statistics for nonbinary folks.) I can assume these numbers may be low, as I can imagine there are sociological reasons for men to underreport their experiences of abuse.

There are often very complex reasons why individuals remain in difficult domestic situations. The National Domestic Violence Hotline says that the most dangerous time for an individual is when they decide to leave an abusive situation.[2] It can be dangerous because perpetrators have been known to snuff out the lives of those who are trying to leave a violent domestic situation. Some clergy and lay leaders might quickly jump to suggest a parishioner leave a violent domestic situation, but the realities of leaving can be dangerous and complicated. In a spiritual-care situation, remember that leaving isn't always the straightforward answer we see as outsiders to the situation.

Domestic violence can also be called "intimate partner violence," but it is not limited to only between two adults. As

---

1   Centers for Disease Control, "Intimate Partner Violence, Sexual Violence, and Stalking Among Men," May 16, 2024, https://www.cdc.gov/intimate-partner -violence/about/intimate-partner-violence-sexual-violence-and-stalking-among -men.html.

2   "Why People Stay," National Domestic Violence Hotline, accessed March 26, 2025, https://www.thehotline.org/support-others/why-people-stay-in-an-abusive -relationship/.

previously mentioned, oftentimes, other family members are experiencing domestic violence within the family system as well. Sometimes, domestic violence includes sexual violence, but it doesn't necessarily always include it. At the time of publication the DOJ said, "domestic violence includes rape, sexual assault, robbery, and aggravated and simple assault committed by intimate partners, immediate family members, or other relatives."[3] So it is essential to know in any care situation that the term "domestic violence" can mean many things.

Tools for Insight: Power and Control Dynamics

One tool that can help in understanding the cycle of abuse can be found in the Power and Control Wheel, published and copyrighted by the Domestic Abuse Intervention Project.[4] The Power and Control Wheel illustrates different methods of abuse and control. It is also a valuable tool in analyzing a given situation. It may also function as an informative tool in identifying early signs of possible domestic violence before things have escalated. This is a tool that can be used by clergy to analyze and evaluate a given circumstance either during

---

3   US Department of Justice, Bureau of Justice Statistics Special Report, "Nonfatal Domestic Violence, 2003–2012," NCJ 244697, April 17, 2014, https://bjs.ojp.gov /library/publications/nonfatal-domestic-violence-2003-2012.
4   "Power and Control," National Domestic Violence Hotline, accessed March 26, 2025, https://www.thehotline.org/identify-abuse/power-and-control/.

or prior to a pastoral care opportunity. According to the Power and Control Wheel, methods of control and abuse include intimidation, coercion and threats, emotional abuse, economic abuse, male privilege, using children, minimizing and blaming, and isolation. These red flags may be instructive when walking alongside a parishioner.

When we consider the realities of domestic violence, we may find some insight in looking at another wheel called the Wheel of Privilege. In some situations, just naming the reality of a dangerous situation may be what a parishioner needs. Accurate naming is essential, and it is validating but also fraught with difficult emotions such as denial, fear, and anxiety. The Wheel of Power and Control can offer us and the abused insight into the current situation and vulnerabilities of the person you serve and walk alongside. This tool can be invaluable for clergy who are unfamiliar with the study of power or who may be unfamiliar with the realities of domestic violence. I find that it helps me put various identities, particularly in a diverse parish setting, into perspective, considering how a person may be more vulnerable to the systems of our society than another.

To understand the possible structures of power and marginality, take a look at the Wheel of Privilege and Power adapted from James R. Vanderwoerd's "Web of Oppression"[5]

5   Found in James Vanderwoerd, "The Promise and Perils of Anti-Oppressive Practice For Christians in Social Work Education," *Social Work and Christianity* 43, no. 2 (July 2016): 153–88.

and Sylvia Duckworth's "Wheel of Power/Privilege."[6] This wheel will also be helpful when we think about religious and spiritual abuse because our role as a clergyperson comes with power and privilege. For our purposes here, you might see what power and marginality exist in the person you are caring for who has experienced or is experiencing domestic violence. I'd encourage you to look at this wheel of power and privilege and first analyze your identity. What identifying markers make you more or less privileged? Then, you might consider looking at this same wheel for a parishioner to try to understand the power dynamics at play. It is likely that with more access to power and privilege, you may have an easier time moving out of a domestic-violence situation than other identities. You may have access to resources, relationships, and community members that would make domestic violence more manageable. This analysis can help both clergy and lay leaders navigate diverse parishes and allow you to be mindful of presuppositions you may carry or actions you take for granted due to your own identity.

Pastoral Roles: Supporting in Crisis and Beyond

There are two separate places where churches, priests, and parish leaders may become involved or informed about a

---

6   Wheel of Power/Privilege, by Sylvia Duckworth for the Canadian Council of Refugees (CCR), https://ccrweb.ca/en/anti-oppression.

domestic-violence situation. First, there is the moment
of crisis when a person is looking for help for an ongoing
problem. In these moments of crisis, the pastoral imperative
is to walk alongside them in naming the situation, validating
their experiences, and seeking to get them the help they
need. Particularly amid a crisis, we, as clergy, are to care for
a person's soul. Encourage them to find a good therapist,
reach out to a social worker, or report the abuse if that is the
best course of action. Remember that they chose to speak
with you, which may have been a big decision that took great
courage.

Secondly, there is another way to think about domestic
violence in parishes, and that is for those who have experienced domestic harm *in the past*. This is where support groups
and lay leaders come into the equation. In this case, the abuse
isn't an ongoing feature of their current lives, and sometimes,
these stories of past harm are more prevalent because there
may be less immediate shame and embarrassment than in a
situation that is currently taking place. The same norms for
validating one's experiences and providing space to tell their
story are all appropriate forms of support for those who have
suffered intimate partner violence in the past.

I want to say something about divorce because there is
a long history in the Christian church of denying women,
and perhaps men as well, the autonomy to divorce someone.
After all, marriage is a sacramental or spiritual rite. Still, this
kind of theological principle—that divorce is a sin—is not

well-founded in Scripture and, in my opinion, crosses the line into spiritual or religious abuse. But seeing divorce as a sin can still permeate progressive contexts, even if unintentionally.

In cases of domestic violence, I believe it is decidedly immoral to imply or convey that divorce is unrighteous. Divorce in cases of intimate partner violence should be affirmed and offered as an essential step forward. There may be some spiritual healing that has to occur before a person can take that step due to decades of false teachings on divorce. Of course, each situation is complex, and you must be mindful of the other dynamics. Are the authorities involved? Are there kids involved? Does someone have the socioeconomic resources to file for divorce? Are kids being abused too? These are not questions you need answers to, but they are essential pieces of this complex puzzle of domestic violence.

Mandated Reporting: Guidelines and Challenges

I grieve the systems that fail to protect the vulnerable—the silence of the church, the apathy of society, and the laws that leave too many without refuge. However, a pastoral segment on domestic violence would not be complete without straightforward, practical suggestions for mandated reporting. Mandated reporting applies primarily to licensed clergy.

Mandated reporting is complicated because the systems and laws in place may not be able to help families in the way that many involved may have hoped. As I've mentioned earlier in this book, clergy should be very clear about mandated reporting expectations and requirements and make those expectations very clear to any parishioner seeking your spiritual care at the outset of your conversation. I always stop a parishioner early in a conversation to tell them I will always keep confidentiality unless a child or another person is currently being hurt. In cases like this, clergy are mandated reporters.

Know your local laws and the expectations of your denomination or church. If you are unsure whether to report something, immediately consult someone who can offer you good guidance.

If mandated reporting does have to occur, be aware that you will give the situation to the authorities. For better or for worse, you may remain out of the remainder of the process. It could depend on your depth of knowledge of the situation. There can be many challenges for the household at this moment in the crisis, particularly for families where imminent danger or loss of life is a very real possibility. Providing other types of support, such as daily meals or activities for the children during lawyers' or other essential meetings, could offer relief to families.

Another tip for mandated reporting is to invite the parishioner into the processes. Perhaps you can schedule a time to make the report together, explain the necessity and requirements as a mandated reporter, and invite them into the conversation when you can. Doing so can bring more profound understanding, companionship, and support for a difficult situation.

I strongly urge you always to be gentle, affirming, and validating. Understand that leaving the relationship doesn't always seem like a viable option to the abused. Without all the information, you will have no idea if it is. In many cases, you do not even need all of the information (because that is not your role).

Additional Resources: In the Media

If domestic violence is very unfamiliar to you, I'd strongly urge you to watch the series entitled *Unbelievable* on Netflix. It is a dramatic limited series based on actual events, and it highlights some of the realities of reporting sexual abuse. While the plot isn't technically domestic abuse, it accurately and brilliantly reveals what a survivor must go through in reporting abuse and some of the legalities that make it so challenging. You will notice that in many ways the criminal justice system is not set up to care for the spiritual and emotional well-being of individuals, which makes sense given that that isn't their goal. In my opinion, that is where spiritual caregivers can come in with God's grace, God's anguish at the situation, and God's unending love for the abused.

Spiritual caregivers, including lay leaders and clergy, can be a significant source of support. They can offer to accompany or drive a person to a rape-kit appointment or simply be a supportive presence throughout the complex process. If you can handle the Netflix series' challenging content, I strongly recommend it to clergy and lay leaders because it can give you a clearer view of what complicates the reporting process. While getting the authorities involved may be necessary, it is still one of the most challenging journeys a person may have to endure.

Another Netflix dramatic series that offers an excellent depiction of the difficulty of leaving a domestic-violence situation is *Maid*. *Maid* follows the life of a young mother who escapes her abusive life and draws special attention to socio-economic struggles. It shows the realities of a women's shelter, the financial challenges for many single women in caring for their children and earning an income, and the challenge of caring for a young child amid this type of legal drama.

Prayer and Spiritual Practices

The following prayers can be used in a care situation by clergy or church leaders who are walking with individuals who carry the burden of domestic violence. Feel free to use this and alter it to fit your situation. I have intentionally written this prayer free from victim-blaming and with a personal knowledge of some of the complexities of domestic violence. You might also use this prayer in your own prayer time for a parishioner. I like to use the ritual of lighting a candle to set the tone. It's an embodied act that helps me remember to welcome God's spirit. I strongly urge you to find a ritual that works for you. I have intentionally worded this prayer to shift the weight to the community. It is in the community that one can begin to find the resources and relationships to exit a domestic-violence situation.

In my view, the most important role of a clergyperson or church leader is to validate, validate, validate. When someone feels safe enough to share their experiences, it is essential to remain nonjudgmental and validate the feelings and experiences of those who are abused. If your instinct is to make a judgment about someone else's choices, you may not be able to come alongside someone in this situation safely. Please check your privilege because, as mentioned previously, domestic violence can intersect with many forms of power and marginality.

In these care situations I have found it increasingly important to remember that I cannot want something for parishioners more than they want it for themselves. This adage applies to domestic violence, too. The care seeker must want to take steps to change their situation for themselves. I have come to notice how my wanting wholeness for them isn't the same thing as them wanting it for themselves. Furthermore, you may not have all the information about what makes a domestic-violence situation volatile. Remember, choosing to leave a partner who has caused intimate partner violence can be dangerous. Be sure to refrain from any victim blaming! Your role is to validate, validate, validate!

A Prayer for Lament and Intercession— Domestic Violence

God of compassion, we cry out in lament. For all those who suffer the pain of domestic violence. For the fear they endure, the harm they have suffered, and the isolation that keeps them lonely, we lament. Merciful Lord, we grieve the brokenness of homes meant to reflect your love and peace. Where injustice has prevailed, bring your justice. Where lives are shattered, bring your healing. Be present, O Lord, with all who carry these heavy burdens, and move us by your Spirit to be instruments of your hope, safety, and restoration. Through Jesus Christ our Lord, who lives and reigns with you and the Holy Spirit, one God, now and forever. Amen.

Chapter 7

Racial Trauma Primer

In her book *Resurrecting Wounds*, Shelley Rambo opens her chapter on Christian theology and racism with this: "The wounds of racism live under the surface of our collective skin."[1] Her imagery reminds me of how deep this type of trauma runs and how it branches out to impact our communities in many ways.

I must situate this chapter in the context of Black Christian thinkers who have been writing about racial trauma for decades. James Cone, Howard Thurman, Martin Luther King Jr., Willie Jennings, and Paul Lawrence Dunbar are just some of these thinkers who contributed massive amounts of theological thinking on the Christian church and race.

Howard Thurman's mention of overt racism is just as relevant today as it was during Thurman's time. He says,

---

1   Rambo, *Resurrecting Wounds*, 71.

During the early days of the war I noticed a definite rise in rudeness and overt expressions of color prejudice, especially in trains and other public conveyances. It was very simple; hatred could be brought out into the open, given a formal dignity and a place of respectability.[2]

These words don't sound far off to me; they sound distinctly relatable and relevant for this moment. Howard Thurman wrestles with whether there is anything of value for the disinherited, the weak, the poor, the social outcast, within the religion of Jesus.[3] I'd like to believe there certainly is, but acknowledging the realities of what it means to be a Christian church made up of many races and a history of colonization is important.

In fact, James Cone reminds us that the cross can both heal and hurt. He says, "It can be empowering and liberating but also enslaving and oppressive. There is no one way in which the cross can be interpreted."[4] Because like virtually any religious symbol it can be used to offer hope to the oppressed or cause more harm.

Mental Health America calls racial trauma "race-based traumatic stress."[5] Race-based traumatic stress (RBTS) can be described using five main categories.

---

2 Thurman, *Jesus and the Disinherited*, 64.
3 Thurman, *Jesus and the Disinherited*, 36.
4 Cone, *The Cross and Lynching Tree*.
5 "Racial Trauma," Mental Health America, accessed March 26, 2025, https://www.mhanational.org/racial-trauma.

- Direct experience with racism
  - Such as being racially profiled or experiencing a hate crime.
- Vicarious trauma
  - Witnessing a traumatic instance of racism such as police violence. This can hold deep impact for those who hold the same identity as the victim.
- Systemic and institutional racism
  - Experiencing the ongoing impact of systems of oppression in our modern world, such as unfair hiring practices or being racially profiled in the hiring process.
- Intergenerational trauma
  - This includes racial trauma that impacts families for generations, much like the example of Kalaupapa in chapter 4.
- Microaggressions
  - The subtle and subversive racist comments that BIPOC (Black, Indigenous, and People of Color) folks experience everyday throughout their daily lives.

I write from my own perspective as a non-Black person of color. My experiences will differ significantly from those of Black and Indigenous individuals. I am the proud daughter of a Colombian immigrant and a white mother.

About ten years ago, I attended a required church conference for work. It was the first time I had ever heard race addressed in that kind of setting—and it struck a deep emotional chord. I remember coming home and weeping. For the first time, someone spoke publicly about the challenges of race and identity within the Christian church. I hadn't realized until that moment how much I had longed to see people who looked like me leading our congregations and shaping our denominations. That moment marked the beginning of my own process of decolonizing my faith and my mind. It was also when I began to fully claim my identity as a biracial pastor—even if not everyone saw me that way (many assumed I was white).

The conversation overwhelmed me. It felt personal and urgent. For the first time, I felt seen. But at the same time, it awakened something in me. It brought a flood of long-buried racial trauma to the surface. And as the only biracial person in my church—and on the pastoral staff—I felt incredibly alone in the journey.

As a biracial woman, every time race came up in staff meetings or church discussions, I felt like two parts of myself were at war. It was as though the divisions tearing through our country had found their way into my own body. The white and nonwhite parts of myself felt locked in conflict, reflecting back the polarization all around me.

Now, years later, I feel like I'm making up for lost time. The best advice I can give is this: surround yourself with culturally competent people. That's what I try to do now. I seek out people who can help me understand my own racial identity and the trauma it carries.

I haven't fully unraveled my complicated relationship with ethnicity and whiteness—it's something I'm still working through. Maybe one day I'll be ready to write more about it. For many of us who are biracial, identity can be deeply complex. There's still a lack of robust psychological research focused specifically on biracial populations. Most studies center either white experiences or Black experiences. But the human experience is far more nuanced—there's a wide spectrum that still needs to be seen, studied, and understood. That includes the stories of non-Black people of color too.

Racial Trauma for People of Color

Racial trauma is complex, particularly for people of color. Each culture has its own history of trauma. When I was working at a church in California, we would often hear stories of the Japanese Americans who were interned in camps in California during World War II. When I was at a church in Hawaii, we talked about the Indigenous people who were torn away from their families and home for the creation of the governmental land—the Kalaupapa leprosy colony in the nineteenth century. When I was in North Carolina attending graduate school, we talked about the land that was tilled by enslaved African peoples. The histories of each of these groups are unique and different, and thus the impact of various racial traumas and intergenerational trauma will be different.

If you are a person of color, you are likely incredibly resilient and able to manage the bombardment of white-body supremacy everywhere in our world. Truthfully, I bristle at the word "resilient," mostly because you shouldn't have to be. Resilience is birthed out of trauma! And yet, resilience is like a superpower. Your ability to survive and even thrive despite historic injustice and mistreatment is an incredibly brave act. Resmaa Menakem explains, "resilience is built into the cells of our bodies. Like trauma, resilience can ripple outward, changing the lives of people, families, neighborhoods, and communities in positive ways. Also like trauma, resilience can be passed down from generation to generation."[6] Menakem's outlook gives us hope that resilience has a place in this conversation for healing racial trauma.

I want to leave you with two practical books by social workers in the field that may be helpful for a variety of people of color. The first is my recommendation to work through Menakem's book, *My Grandmother's Hands: Racialized Trauma and the Pathway to Mending our Hearts and Bodies.*

In this book, he includes somatic exercises and ancestral work, and explores many therapeutic concepts in relation to racialized trauma for both white bodies and black and brown bodies. He explains how his work is built upon the idea of "post-traumatic slave syndrome," which is a concept that Dr. Joy DeGruy developed. This is what he has to say about

---

6   Menakem, *My Grandmother's Hands*, 55.

that foundational work: "She looks in detail at the violence and abuse inflicted on enslaved African people in America; at the continued abuse inflicted on their descendants; and at how this trauma has been passed down—and continues to be passed down—through generation upon generation of African Americans."[7] Menakem's practical methodologies are helpful for any amount of racial harm and seek to help individuals unpack racial trauma that may have been passed down from generation to generation.

Menakem also explores the concept of secondary trauma or vicarious trauma, resilience, generational trauma, and white-body supremacy. He is laser-focused on mind-body practices for this specific type of trauma which can help to mend the mind-body relationship.

Tips:

For clergy, *My Grandmother's Hands* by Resmaa Menakem is another good book to have on hand because it can be offered as a therapeutic intervention in pastoral care situations. He is an expert in racialized trauma and can be one resource for individuals who may not have access to the right type of therapist, whether it be due to lack of access to a therapist or lack of the therapist's ability to engage with the topic.

---

7 Menakem, *My Grandmother's Hands*, 58.

But What Will People Say? Navigating Mental Health, Identity, Love and Family Between Cultures by Sahaj Kaur Kohli is another excellent resource for children of immigrants and second-generation folks who wish to understand and unpack racial trauma.

Kohli explores diverse psychosocial concepts such as assimilation, enculturation, and integration. People of color (POC) may find a new lens to understand their experiences from growing up with immigrant parents, or they may notice differences between first and second generations in their own family systems. She contemplates all of these complexities in a refreshing way and shares her own personal stories that help illustrate the concepts.

While she is of South Asian descent, the concepts were helpful for my own understanding as a second-generation Latina, having been raised by a Colombian immigrant father and a white mother. Although even my biological culture (Singaporean) plays a role in the cultural framework of my upbringing.

As mentioned previously, bicultural identity is an area that is deeply underdeveloped in psychosocial research. Kohli is one of the first to be so intently attuned to bicultural identity. In fact she says, "I know firsthand the suffering, the questions, the inconsistencies, and the inner torment that come with trying to occupy two spaces at once, with having no sense of belonging to one or the other and needing to chart a path forward anyway."[8] I find her work deeply relatable, as both a biracial person and a person who grew up with an immigrant father. She acknowledges that sometimes two cultures are in conflict and we still have to understand the full context of who we are in the midst of multicultural influences.

Tip:

For clergy, once again, I'd recommend keeping this book close by as another pastoral intervention for those who have questions about race and faith, especially for those who grew up in constraining and restrictive religious cultures. After all, understanding their own identities may bring beauty and clarity to their relationship with God as they understand themselves even better.

Positive Religious Coping
Versus Negative Religious Coping

This may be self-explanatory to some readers, but for those who were raised by immigrant parents with strict religious dogma, Kohli helpfully differentiates between positive religious coping and negative religious coping. Positive religious coping takes into account that a given religious leader or support system can "increase self-esteem as it relates to being part of something larger than oneself, and it can enhance

---

8 Kohli, *But What Will People Say*, 4.

prosocial behaviors in religious and cultural communities."[9] This is what we seek in our congregations.

However, some people have a very different experience with the faith of their families. What parishes can do is seek to avoid negative religious coping, which is the notion that "centers the idea that God is punishing or abandoning us whenever we make mistakes or have negative experiences."[10] If this is the type of religion you are used to or that you grew up with, I want to encourage you to look at Kohli's work. There are many churches, denominations, and individual congregations who will affirm your identity and self-understanding. Do not give up on finding the right place for you.

For White Readers

But what is a little harder to write about is white-body supremacy. As I understand it, racial trauma affects *every* race. Whether you are the perpetrator of harm or the receiver of harm, racial trauma impacts the souls of all involved. It dehumanizes everyone, placing one type of person above and over the other, even if unintentionally. It's a disordered view of humanity, even if only a subconcious disordering.

The following section is especially for white allies. I have some perspective having navigated both my white racial

---

9   Kohli, *But What Will People Say*, 134.
10   Kohli, *But What Will People Say*, 134.

identity and my Colombiana racial identity. The number one thing that I have found most helpful from white allies is their awareness of their own white racial identity. If you are able to do the work to become clear about what it means for you to be white it will help you understand how to come alongside others accepting your own identity fully.

White racial literacy isn't as scary as it sounds but it does take time and like any other identity it may take a lifetime to understand it fully. Like many things in our faithful lives as Christians, anti-racist work requires a lifelong commitment.

Like my previous chapters, I will offer some practical suggestions for how churches might be places that bring about deeper healing and reconciliation, reducing moments of harm and fostering a place of healing for all.

In our baptismal vows, we commit to honoring the dignity of every human being. If you are white and you decide to skip this chapter because you don't think it impacts you, you have missed my point because racial trauma causes harm to both white and nonwhite people. I urge you to continue reading! In this chapter, I will address my white audience first, then I will address racial trauma for BIPOC (Black, Indigenous, People of Color) individuals more specifically.

Racial Trauma: for Allies

Racial trauma affects the perpetrator, even if one doesn't recognize it right away. Racial harm, like any other harm, is a sin. When we sin, we cause harm not only to others but to ourselves. But the interesting thing about causing harm to another is that one actually dehumanizes themself as well as the other person. The dual impact of racial sin isn't something one can get away from; we all do it, and we all hurt others and ourselves in the process. Christ's call is to reconcile, ask for forgiveness, partake of the sacraments, receive absolution, and restore to each other the dignity we all deserve.

But you may be wondering how and why racial trauma impacts a white person. Let me explain. One harmful experience I have encountered is the idea that some white people quickly assume that their way of seeing the world is universal, or in even starker terms, the "right" way to see the world. This is a form of white supremacy.

Robin DiAngelo wrote an excellent work on White Racial Literacy. She is a social psychologist and her words are powerful. She says,

> While I am aware that race has been used unfairly against people of color, I haven't been taught to see that as *my* problem, as long as I personally haven't done anything wrong. This actually affords me a level of racial relaxation and emotional and intellectual space that people of color are not afforded as they navigate mainstream society.[11]

---

11   DiAngelo, *What Does It Mean to Be White*, 177–178.

The damage caused to BIPOC individuals may be more obvious, but when a person propagates ideas of whiteness as standard, it harms the person of the dominant culture as well, making them believe their perspective is indeed universal. This inflated sense of self can become destructive, distorting their understanding of humanity and connection with others.

It also causes harm in other, very practical ways. It harms collaborative communication, breaks trust between people, and causes racial trauma toward others. While white-body supremacy is a sin, it is a sin we can recover from or at least try to recover from.

Now of course white-body supremacy causes harm to people of color. At its most impactful it dehumanizes, and at its least impactful it excludes diverse voices. But it also impacts the internal lives of these same people. It can cause BIPOC folks to question their points of view and to doubt that their perceptions are fair and valuable. Resmaa Menakem says

> Race is a myth—something made up in the seventeenth century that has been carried forward, day by day, century after century, into the present . . . It's a classic example of what therapists call *gaslighting*: getting people to override their own experience and perceptions by repeating a lie over and over and then "proving" it with still more lies, denials, and misdirection.[12]

12 Menakem, *My Grandmother's Hands*, 67–68.

Resmaa is clear that race being a myth does not mean it has no impact on us now. People of color may begin to believe other lies about themselves and their identity due to this form of gaslighting.

This can also be known as internalized oppression. Internalized oppression is when a person comes to internalize oppressive prejudices and biases about the identity group to which he/she/they belong.

Tip:

Perhaps consider hosting an affinity group for LGBTQ+ folks and/or BIPOC folks. Sometimes, these kinds of affinity groups can offer a safe place of understanding and companionship. Helping folks to find one another within your parish community can be a powerful tool for healing.

When the rhetoric around immigrants in 2015 became imbued with language that "all" Latinos were "rapists," I found myself searching for a spiritual home that would protect me and others from this kind of rhetoric. I worried about what others thought of me and feared that other parishioners might believe that I or my people were dangerous. It is evident to me now that I was experiencing a form of internalized oppression. I had come to believe certain things about myself, and I feared what others believed about me.

But these fears were mostly contrived from public rhetoric rather than actual treatment within my parish. The impact of internalized oppression was still very real.

Tip:

If you find that public mainstream rhetoric is impacting you negatively, I strongly recommend you take a break from that particular type of media. Being bombarded with false messages about the group you belong to is harmful to your psychological health. Much of our media is a cesspool for racism—this concept actually applies to other identities such as LGBTQ+ individuals as well—and so I encourage you to take a break from social media and other places where toxic and untrue ideologies are perpetuated.

White-Body Supremacy Is Like an Addiction

This next section may be challenging for white readers. If you are white, I encourage you to keep reading. If you consider yourself an ally, or wish to be one, I hope you can find ways you can support your BIPOC peers and congregants here.

For both the perpetrator and the victim, racial trauma exists. It exists in different capacities and has a different role and function for each. I'd like to argue that white-body supremacy (for any race) is like an addiction. At this juncture, it may be important to explain that even BIPOC individuals may find white-body supremacy attractive, however subconsciously. Let me explain.

For those of us who can "pass as white," like myself, our everyday lives often ask us to be "more white," that is, become more like white people and white culture. I may think, "if I can behave just a little bit more like my white peers, I can fit in, I can assimilate, I can succeed." Or maybe even, "I can survive." Perhaps you've heard the pervasive experience of many personal stories from young brown children trying to wipe off their brown skin tone, desiring to be like their white counterparts to fit in, to survive, to belong.

White-body supremacy is pervasive and deeply embedded within our culture. It impacts us all and in some ways there are overlaps between white-body supremacy and any other addiction. Below I have written twelve steps for recovering from white-body supremacy. This is a lifelong journey that requires us to receive Christ's grace as we engage with these steps.

Twelve Steps of Recovery for White Allies

Because of the pervasive nature of white-body supremacy, I have taken the twelve steps from Alcoholics Anonymous and refracted them through the concept of racial harm and white-body supremacy. These are my own twelve steps to recovering from white-body supremacy. I have found it helpful to understand my own journey in these steps and my prayer is that you will too.

- Step One: Admit Powerlessness
We acknowledge that it is by God's grace that we can heal from white-body supremacy. It is so deeply embedded in our lives and way of thinking that only God can give us grace and power to change our thoughts and actions. The first step is to realize racial injustice exists and that you have very little control over squelching it on your own. This step is a reminder that this work is more effective when it's done in community.

- Step Two: Rely on God's Power
One of the well-known features of Alcoholics Anonymous and many other twelve-step programs is the Serenity Prayer. The Serenity Prayer is first associated with a sermon by Richard Niebuhr in 1943. Alcoholics Anonymous later adapted it to their program, and many programs still recite it today at their meetings. It's a prayer that reminds us that we do not change on our own, it is through God's grace that we can begin to make dramatic changes in our lives.

- Step Three: Align Yourself with God's Purposes
We worship a God who wants to see reconciliation and wholeness, unity in our diversity. Be brave in this work.

• Step Four: Take Inventory

You may want to start with the book *Blindspot: Hidden Biases of Good People* by Mahzarin R. Banaji and Anthony G. Greenwald. Take the implicit bias assessment. Use other tools to evaluate and take inventory, such as any of Robin DiAngelo's work on white racial literacy. This will give you further insight into your own thought patterns and give you a foundation for where to begin more work.

• Step Five: Confess and Acknowledge Harm

When I'm in the throes of white-body supremacy nothing brings me more hope than praying our Confession of Sin from Rite II. It is a prayer of confession where we ask God to forgive us for the things we have done and the things we have left undone. We also ask for forgiveness for the things that have been done on our behalf. The phrase "The things we have left undone" from the BCP confession, when refracted through this conversation on white-body supremacy, makes me think of the moments I didn't use my privilege to stand up for others. Even if it was by my unconscious white-body supremacy. In part, the unconsciousness of white-body supremacy is part of the challenge, and a significant reason why we needs God's forgiveness. "The things done on our behalf" makes me think of all the unseen privileges I experience because of the systems of white-body supremacy. This acknowledgment of sin makes room for the moments when those around me assume I'm white and the unearned privileges and assumptions that I earn because of it. Even if they go unnoticed on a daily basis. Once again, I have little control over that, and this is why we need God's forgiveness. There is an interesting balance between personal responsibility and God's ability to forgive all our sins, even the ones we overlook in ourselves. It is only by confession and right relationship with Christ that we receive the Holy Eucharist as one form of God's love and inclusion, regardless of our sin.

- Step Six: Be Ready to Change

Be ready to make changes, to upset the status quo, and to bring others along with you on your journey. Don't rush these steps and don't assume they will happen in a day or a week. This is lifelong work; I recommend making small and practical changes first.

- Step Seven: Ask God for Transformation

Let the Eucharist be your guide. Christ welcomes you at his table no matter what shortcomings exist. In fact, each week we humbly kneel and receive Christ's free gift for all.

- Step Eight: Identify Those You've Harmed

Please notice that this is just the first step for making amends. Make a full and complete list but don't do anything with that list quite yet. You can keep this for your own personal growth, prayer, confession, and reflection.

• Step Nine: Make Amends Thoughtfully

If someone has come to you with a racial harm you have perpetrated you may want to go back after you've done some of this work and make amends. Bear in mind that if a person of color comes to a white person to speak directly of a racial harm they likely see possibility for greater understanding and mutual respect. (I think I can safely say, based on my personal experience, that many people of color will simply choose not to bother raising the topic unless they believe some kind of reconciliation is possible.)

If the harm is toward a parishioner you will need to prayerfully consider if making amends is the best course of action. It is possible that with the power dynamic between clergy and parishioner making amends may not be useful depending on how much time has elapsed and the nature of the relationship. If there is a possibility to retraumatize someone I would recommend to err on the side of caution.

In the parish setting, as clergy, I'd encourage you to decenter your own experience and center the other when discerning. You may want to consider: could this be helpful to the parishioner, or cause further harm? Are you doing it to make yourself feel better? Ask yourself what the other person might need. Try to center the other's experience instead of your own experience when possible.

- Step Ten: Continue Self-Reflection

Once again, this step reminds us that this is a process. It acknowledges that we all make mistakes and even with good intentions the impact of our words and actions can cause harm. Be quick to apologize.

- Step Eleven: Deepen Your Spiritual Connection

Get plugged into a group such as Sacred Ground in the Episcopal Church or an affinity group that cares about social justice and dismantling white-body supremacy. Try to find these individuals within your church so you can make spiritual connections together. Pray the Confession of Sin together and hold one another accountable. Use prayer and meditation to improve your connection with God.

- Step Twelve: Commit to Lifelong Practice

Shedding our white-body supremacy is a lifelong practice. No one expects your perfection but continue to prioritize dismantling white-body supremacy in your own life and the communities you interact with.

Prayer for Racial Justice for a Mixed-Race Group

Creator, Redeemer, Sustainer, you see us living in an increasingly divided and challenging world. Give us the ability to understand the impact of racial trauma in our own lives and give us the ability to devise new insights about our beliefs and behaviors. We acknowledge that you have created each person with their own unique point of view and a distinct voice. Where we have caused pain, we ask for your forgiveness and the clarity to mend relationships. Where we have doubted our own experiences and perceptions, give us strength to know the truth. Guide us in your way of love to honor and uphold the dignity of all your people. Give us access to your inheritance of healing. Through Christ our Lord, Amen.

Chapter 8

Spiritual and Religious Abuse Primer

Introduction: Naming the Wound

If you understand what it's like to live in fundamentalist evangelical fear, I want you to know that I see you. The fear in my childhood was palpable. Being a child, all alone, separated from God, because of my sin. Wondering if I would be *left behind* at the time of the rapture, when my family would float up into the heavens. Would my faith have failed, and would I be left without *mi familia*?

When I dared to step outside my religious past, some family members disowned me. The phone calls stopped; the invitations stopped. Suddenly, there was a vast chasm in my relationships. My calling to the priesthood was seen not just as rebellion, but as heresy. I felt as though I had to grieve my loss of family, even though they were still alive.

If this is familiar, I want you to know you are not alone. I see you! I've come to believe that just because someone can't see me clearly doesn't mean I'm unworthy of love. True, deep, abiding love, God's love, doesn't rely on fear. If my own family's love had to be bought with conformity, then it wouldn't have sustained me anyway.

This kind of spiritual abuse, or other similar forms, is where I will spend most of our time in the chapter ahead.

Defining Spiritual and Religious Abuse

Spiritual and religious abuse is any abuse that is perpetrated in the name of God or in the name of a spiritual leader. Abuses can range from illegal acts, such as abusing a child, to theological and spiritual acts, such as destructive theology. My focus is on the latter. Although it is helpful to understand that I am mostly interested in creating a culture of radical welcome within a parish community that makes room for, acknowledges, and supports someone's experience with past religious trauma.

Some religious leaders may use Scripture or their spiritual authority to control members. When members have been harmed by destructive religious leaders, it can leave parishioners with a loss of trust, identity struggles, religious trauma, and even PTSD symptoms.

I know of other ex-evangelicals who have experienced abuses such as volunteerism to the point of exploitation.

Others were traumatized by abstinence teachings like the purity culture story I shared at the beginning of this book. Yet others experienced total and complete authority of an institution in their life.

These are all examples of spiritual and religious abuse. Part of what makes this kind of trauma so impactful is that our spiritual lives and what we believe about God are bound up with a painful experience. This can discolor one's understanding of God's love and grace.

Even the realization that a religious institution has been abusive can be disorienting. People may have to contend with losing their communities by leaving an abusive church. They may question their relationship with God and wonder if their religious experiences were even real.

The Church's Role in Repairing Harm

If you are reading this book, I'm assuming you are part of or seeking to be part of a welcoming and affirming community. You may have or will have a parishioner who has experienced spiritual and religious abuse in the past. Please take care not to retraumatize individuals, even if unintentionally.

As in other sections of this book, clergy and lay leaders can seek to name and validate when someone expresses religious or spiritual abuse. Some survivors might struggle to believe their pain is indeed real. Even something like "church hurt" can be considered real trauma.

Many of the tools and practices shared in the earlier pages of this book could support survivors within your community.

- Open up a support group for survivors of spiritual abuse where they can find safe community (use the guidelines I shared in chapter 3).
- Use practical and embodied religious practices (also mentioned in previous chapters)
- Explain the background behind a particular religious practice or liturgical decision; transparency will provide additional safety to individuals
- Invite questions and pushback on theological concepts

Deconstruction and Recovering from Harmful Theology

Healing from harmful theology is a journey that unfolds in two main stages. The first is deconstruction—a process of questioning, unlearning, and critically examining the theological beliefs that may have caused harm. This stage takes time, so allow yourself patience and grace. Grief is often an inevitable part of this process, as you come to terms with beliefs that once shaped your identity and worldview.

Many ex-evangelicals and survivors of religious trauma find themselves deconstructing the following theological ideas:

- Purity culture and gender roles
  - The toxic belief that women belong in the home while men belong in the workforce.
  - Women who are unable to conceive are especially theologically vulnerable.
- Fear-based faith
  - A faith that relies on the threat of hell or other forms of judgment to control and manipulate believers.
- Rapture or End Times terror
  - The specific theological belief that the Second Coming of Christ is near and will come in a literal sense, wherein believers will be taken up into the sky/heavens, leaving the unbelievers behind to survive the time of tribulation (or hell on earth).
- Hell theology
  - The theological view that our behavior can permanently separate us from God in the afterlife, often used to create an environment of fear.
- Total Depravity
  - The theological idea that all humanity is born totally depraved, often tied to problematic theologies of original sin.
- Condemnation of LGBTQ+ identities/biblical sexuality
  - Especially in keeping LGBTQ+ individuals out of leadership and membership due purely to their queer identity.
  - Usually identifies queer identity as a "sin."

- Doctrine of total submission to church leaders
  - High-control groups place a high level of responsibility and decision making on a single leader or small group of leaders.
- Biblical literalism
  - The view that the Bible is the literal words of God, there are no mistakes, and it must be understood literally.
  - There is little understanding of the diversity of cultures, scribe methods, possible human errors, and variety of genres within the biblical scriptures.
- Christian nationalism
  - A view that Christianity is inextricably tied to being American often at the rejection of other faith traditions such as Islam, Judaism, and Eastern religions.

Part of the process for survivors of religious and spiritual abuse includes first dismantling (or deconstructing) the bad theology that has been forced upon the abused. Deconstructing is a very important part of the healing, and clergy and lay leaders should welcome this stage. I have found that progressive Christian circles have proven to be a safe place to unpack and unlearn these harmful beliefs. Those who are deconstructing may be looking for:

- A place to process and ask honest theological questions
  - One of the most healing things about my experience with progressive Episcopal priests is their willingness to

help me think about what I believe. Many have asked me questions or pressed me to articulate my ideas which can and has consistently helped me to uncover harmful areas in my own theology.

- A support system that can affirm their experiences and suffering
  - Parish communities can offer companionship and validation as they get to know those who have been spiritually or religiously abused.
- New religious practices and traditions that can inform their renewed sense of faith
  - Grounding folks in something constructive can be helpful. New religious practices can offer a practical reframe for their newfound relationship with their faith and Christ.
- Historicity of these faith practices
  - History can also ground those who have experienced religious abuse in a long tradition; it can remind folks that we are part of something much bigger than just ourselves or even our religious abuse. Being part of a historic tradition offers something like an extended family throughout history.

Reconstructing Faith

The progressive Christian church has an opportunity to play a healing role by offering a safe space to reconstruct one's faith, too. Reconstruction is the next phase of healing from this type of religious and spiritual abuse. Some people may choose not to reconstruct their faith and that is okay. But for those who do choose to, the church can seek to meet folks where they are at.

A big part of my own reconstruction has been learning to trust myself. If something doesn't feel right spiritually I know to trust my intuition and believe myself. This type of trust doesn't come easily, especially for those who are leaving high-control religious groups. At first, I would notice my intuition *after* a situation or circumstance, then I started to be able to notice my intuition in the moment, now I have a strong sense of my own spiritual intuition.

Those who experienced religious or spiritual abuse may find it helpful to rely on a spiritual director who can help you unwind and reflect back to you what might be happening in your spiritual life. A spiritual director can offer you spiritual feedback in a way that is gentle, compassionate, and not as a form of control.

There are networks of spiritual directors throughout the country. If you are looking for a spiritual director your local Episcopal priest might be able to help you get connected to an organization or institution that offers this type of service and companionship.

My spiritual director calls herself a "spiritual companion." I love that title. It captures everything that I would hope to be true about healthy spiritual direction free from coercion, fear, or control. I recommend finding a spiritual director who can reflect back to you what they are seeing and hearing from you and God.

Another helpful way to reconstruct one's faith is to focus one's energy on finding meaningful spiritual practices instead of trying to get all of one's theology correct. For some folks, letting go of theological binaries may be difficult at first but ultimately freeing and necessary, depending on their past religious abuse. Some may want to review the journal exercises in chapter 2 to help find a spiritual practice that you would like to try.

Reconstructing your faith may take time, and it will likely not be a linear enterprise. I want to leave you with a few books for further reading. Some of these fall within the deconstruction category while others may be helpful during your reconstruction.

A Service of Healing

The Episcopal Book of Common Prayer contains a section entitled "Ministration to the Sick."[1] This is a beautiful service of healing including the ancient tradition of laying on of hands and anointing with oil. Anglicans generally hold that healing in all forms is possible but may not happen in the way we hope or in the time we hope. Many Anglicans understand that some healing may only happen at the time when God

---

1   The Book of Common Prayer (Seabury, 1979), 453.

reconciles this earthly world toward the telos of the entire universe—that is, when Christ comes again.

If your community is building relationships around various traumas and demonstrates a desire to heal, perhaps a service of healing is in order. Part of my hope is to understand this type of worship service as impacting those who are affected by trauma as well, not just physical ailments. It can and should be used for both circumstances.

The Book of Common Prayer divides the service into three main sections: the Ministry of the Word, the Laying on of Hands and Anointing, and the Eucharist. My focus is primarily on the embodied act of laying on of hands and anointing.

The laying on of hands and anointing with oil is tied to the apostolic tradition of Hippolytus of Rome, which can be traced all the way back to circa 215 CE.[2] While many of his writings have not been well preserved, we do have some Roman writings about healing and anointing. Anointing and laying on of hands have come in and out of the historic prayer books but the most recent edition of The Book of Common Prayer includes many of the most ancient words and traditions.

This can tie those who have experienced religious abuse to a historic tradition that offers deeper spiritual significance beyond simple salvation from hell. These spiritual rituals can

---

2   Marion J. Hatchett, *Commentary on the American Prayer Book* (HarperCollins, 1995), 459.

offer emotional comfort, and psychic healing for those who have experienced this type of abuse.

Tip:

For clergy, if you are noticing your parish or community is in need of spiritual healing, if you notice they may have suffered religious abuse or exploitation, I encourage you to consider a service of healing based on The Book of Common Prayer.

I appreciate the prayer in The Book of Common Prayer for those in pain. This kind of spiritual and religious abuse can cause deep wounds and after excommunication, broken relationships, distrust, and lack of community. This prayer can acknowledge some of the inner wounds for those who suffer. I have adapted it slightly for this specific purpose:

Lord Jesus Christ, be near me in my time of weakness and pain; sustain me by your grace, that my strength and courage may not fail; heal me according to your will; and help me always to believe that what happens to me here is of little account if you hold me in eternal life, my Lord and my God. Amen.[3]

---

3   The Book of Common Prayer (Seabury, 1979), 461.

Conclusion

There is a prayer found within The Book of Common Prayer that has echoed through centuries and is attributed to St. Francis. It is not only a prayer for transformation but also a plea for healing. Before I unpack its distinct relevance to healing let us first sit with the words. It reads as follows:

> Lord, make us instruments of your peace. Where there is hatred, let us sow love; where there is injury, pardon; where there is discord, union; where there is doubt, faith; where there is despair, hope; where there is darkness, light; where there is sadness, joy. Grant that we may not so much seek to be consoled as to console; to be understood as to understand; to be loved as to love. For it is in giving that we receive; it is in pardoning that we are pardoned; and it is in dying that we are born to eternal life. Amen.[1]

I'd like to imagine that if St. Francis were sitting here with us that he might add "Where there is trauma, healing."

---

1   BCP, 833.

Not because it changes the essence of the prayer but because
it brings it into sharper focus for our time. St. Francis lived
among the poor, the outcast, and the downtrodden. In many
ways, his entire life and ministry was a response to suffering in
the world. So it is no surprise to hear the communal nature of
seeking to console over being consoled, understanding others
over needing to be understood: these are both utopic visions
of what genuine community is. To be an instrument of peace
in today's world is to be someone who sees trauma, acknowledges it, and refuses to turn away.

Having been part of the Episcopal Church since 2018, I
realized that one of the most interesting differences between
my culture and Episcopal culture is the difference between
collectivist culture versus individualist culture. Even in
writing this book I found myself oscillating between the two.
According to Kohli, "individualism encourages a person's
independence and personal growth," whereas "collectivism
encourages group cohesion and collaborative growth."[2]
Neither is better or worse, and actually both types of culture
have their up sides and down sides. Truthfully, a blend of the
two seems to be the most balanced way to operate.

I simply write about collectivist culture out of my own
personal experience. It's a culture whose strength is found in
a deep sense of belonging and support. But one struggle with
collectivist culture is that one can attempt to care for a group

---

2   Kohli, 123-125.

at the expense of one's own well-being. Suffice it to say, in a tradition marred by the ultimate version of individualism—colonialism—I see a future for this Christian tradition to continue to foster and develop even more collectivist vision of community. Deep community that can be built up within our parishes.

The distinction became clear to me during my early years within the Episcopal Church. It was a moment when I noticed the cultural difference in action. In my home culture, we don't wait for someone to ask for help; for better or for worse, we show up unannounced, with presence, food, and kinship. But in some Episcopal spaces I noticed a different kind of care: quiet, measured, waiting to be asked for help. Neither is right or wrong but I think we need each other. I think collectivists need a bit of individualism and I think individualists need a bit more collectivism. I can't help but wonder—what if we brought these two instincts together?

Trauma-informed sacred space is about acknowledging past wounds, using creative forms of prayer, and committing to ending the cycles of harm, but it's also about creating a culture of healing. And real healing doesn't happen in isolation. In fact, isolation can be one of the single most harmful things for one's healing. Healing happens in community. Real community that doesn't wait to be asked, that doesn't say, "that's not my business"; real community that insists on saying "we belong to each other."

St. Francis's words already call us to this work: to be instruments of peace, to sow love where there is injury, and hope where there is despair. If we are to take this seriously, then our parishes must become places where we do not simply gather for worship but where we hold space for one another's pain and commit to each other's healing.

The Journey We've Taken

I hope the practical theology shared in these pages has been helpful. More than anything, I hope my words have come across as compassionate, inclusive, nonjudgmental, and supportive. Many of the tools I've shared have profoundly impacted my own life and led me to break cycles within my own family of origin.

This book was written during a tumultuous time in American history. Some have described it as a constitutional crisis or a technological evolution, while others in the mainstream have used words like "oligarchy." Yet, history reminds us that we have endured difficult political seasons before.

While I don't believe that alarmism is a suitable answer, I do recognize that the trauma experienced by the most vulnerable among us will continue to ripple outward, touching the lives of our communities and our parishes. I hope this book has given you new language, a deeper understanding of how trauma shapes our lives, and perhaps even a few models for what pastoral care and practical ministry might look like in these challenging times.

As progressive Christians, I believe we are called to speak up and act in alignment with Christ's mission—to protect the vulnerable and care for the oppressed. In some cases, this work will lead us outward, beyond our parishes and into the wider community. In others, Christ's mission begins right where we are, within the walls of our own churches.

You may be surprised by the depth of vulnerability within your own parish. Among those who worship beside us are individuals facing profound struggles:

- Those grappling with mental health challenges
- Those estranged from their families
- Survivors of climate disasters or gun violence
- Individuals who have lost their nonpartisan federal jobs unjustly
- Those enduring domestic violence in any form
- People unable to earn a sustainable middle-class income
- Those experiencing homophobia, transphobia, or racial trauma
- Immigrants navigating an unfamiliar and often unwelcoming system
- Children, who are among the most vulnerable of all

Trauma is not just something that happens "out there" in the world—it sits beside us, prays beside us, takes

Communion beside us. Yet, the beauty of the Gospel is this: Healing is possible, and it is possible together.

As I wrote this book, I found myself reflecting deeply on my own theology of suffering. I had to wrestle with how I understand my own wounds in light of the healing I have received—both from Christ and from the Christian community that has surrounded me throughout my life.

And it is through the embodied practices of the Church that we encounter Christ's healing. When we gather to receive the body and blood of Christ we physically walk toward a threshold of something that is holy. We hold the bread in our hands and our mouths as we are wrapped in God's infinite love for us. And it's in these very embodied rituals that we can encounter healing within the Body of Christ.

I struggled with what I could say decisively about suffering, but this I know for certain: pain and healing coexist. Yes, suffering can exist without healing, but for those who do experience healing, pain does not simply vanish—it lingers as a scar, a memory, a physical or emotional wound. True healing does not erase pain; it makes room for it.

And perhaps that is what we, as the church, are called to do as well—to create spaces where healing and pain can exist together, where people are not expected to be whole before they are welcomed, and where the love of Christ makes room for every scar.

The Call to Co-create

The Spirit of the Lord is upon me, because he has anointed me to bring good news to the poor. He has sent me to proclaim release to the captives and recovery of sight to the blind, to let the oppressed go free, to proclaim the year of the Lord's favor.

—Luke 4:18–19 NRSV

The very first words in any Bible speak of God's creation. God's creation of the world and all its inhabitants. God's penultimate creation is humankind, the culmination of all God's creation is bound up in the Sabbath day when God rested. God calls creation into being with care and intention, out of love. But out of this act of love God's creative act is also an invitation. An invitation as co-creators. Trees grow leaves, those leaves "create" photosynthesis; and through this process, those leaves create oxygen for all air-breathing animals, amphibians, birds, and humans. So too, the invitation extends to humankind.

Imbued with the ability to co-create alongside God. But co-create what?

Jesus's first public declaration comes to us in Luke 4:18–19 and makes clear what the creation is meant to be and to do: a world shaped by liberation, healing, and justice. Jesus, standing in the synagogue, reads the ancient Scriptures. He doesn't even offer an interpretation, as if the ancient words are sufficient just as they are. He doesn't offer abstract theological ideas but in reciting the Scriptures he names tangible realities—the poor, the captives, the blind, the oppressed.

If we, as people formed in God's image, are called to be co-creators, then our sacred task is not just to preserve what has been but to build what could be. Co-creating with God means aligning ourselves with the work of liberation—not merely receiving the Good News but actively participating in it. In other words, if God is the Creator, then we are builders, shapers, and restorers. The work of co-creating trauma-informed sacred spaces is deeply theological—it is about mirroring God's work of bringing life out of chaos, restoration out of brokenness. We must work to co-create healing on all levels: on the personal level, on a parish level, and on a systemic level. Not all at once: my unbridled hope is that you begin on a personal level first!

However, a church that proclaims "release to the captives" must actively work against systems of oppression. Healing, in a systemic sense, might mean economic justice, racial reconciliation, and policies that protect the most vulnerable. In this sense liberation is not just a spiritual reality, it is material, and communal.

Co-creating sacred spaces of liberation is not easy. It requires disrupting traditions that exclude, challenging systems that harm, and risking the discomfort of transformation. But Jesus himself models this risk—his ministry of liberation was met with resistance, yet he remained faithful to the call.

The promise of co-creation is that God is with us in this work. We are not alone in shaping this world. The Spirit of God that anointed Jesus to proclaim good news is the same Spirit that empowers us today. Every act of justice, every moment of healing, every space that prioritizes love over exclusion brings us even closer to the kingdom of God.

We do not have to have all the answers. We do not have to do it perfectly. But we are called to begin.

I want to encourage you try a few practical things in your parish community. You don't have to take this on all at the same time. Begin with the smallest change first. I encourage you to pray for paths of least resistance to make themselves known to you. Here are a few ideas to get you started:

1. Start by having a conversation—you might consider inviting members of your parish to gather and discuss how trauma has impacted your community. Perhaps it will be obvious, but if it isn't yet obvious, begin to have the conversations.

2. You might consider finding one tangible change your church can make to become more trauma-informed; it could be training the leadership, creating small groups, affinity groups, or support groups, or adjusting certain worship practices.

3. Probably most important, listen deeply. Surround yourself with a variety of voices, including those who are survivors of trauma. And continue to seek and listen to God's Spirit to lead and guide you in all of this work.

I encourage you to remember to reflect often:

1. Where have you seen pain and healing in your own life?
2. How can you contribute to a more trauma-informed sacred space?
3. Who among you needs to hear the words "you belong" today?

Works Cited

Baldwin, James. *Nobody Knows My Name*. Knopf Doubleday, 1993. E-book.

Banaji, Mahzarin R., and Greenwald, Anthony G. *Blindspot: Hidden Biases of Good People*. Random House, 2013.

Cone, James H. *The Cross and the Lynching Tree*. Orbis, 2011.

DiAngelo, Robin J. *What Does It Mean to Be White? Developing White Racial Literacy*. Peter Lang, 2012.

Feelings Wheel. "Feelings Wheel." Accessed January 30, 2025. https://feelingswheel.com/.

Fisher-Stewart, Gayle. *Black and Episcopalian: The Struggle for Inclusion*. Church Publishing, 2022.

Gamber, Jenifer. *My Faith, My Life: A Teen's Guide to the Episcopal Church*. Church Publishing, Inc., 2006.

Hatchett, Marion J. *Commentary on the American Prayer Book*. HarperCollins, 1995.

Jennings, Willie James. *The Christian Imagination: Theology and the Origins of Race*. Yale University Press, 2010.

Jones, Serene. *Trauma and Grace: Theology in a Ruptured World*. Louisville, Ky.: Westminster John Knox Press, 2009.

Kohli, Sahaj Kaur. *But What Will People Say? Navigating Mental Health, Identity, Love, and Family Between Cultures*. Penguin Random House, 2024.

Levine, Peter A., and Ann Frederick. *Waking the Tiger: Healing Trauma: The Innate Capacity to Transform Overwhelming Experiences.* North Atlantic Books, 1997.

Maté, Gabor, and Daniel Maté. *The Myth of Normal: Trauma, Illness, and Healing in a Toxic Culture.* New York: Avery, 2022.

McAdams, D. P. "First We Invented Stories, Then They Changed Us: The Evolution of Narrative Identity." *Evolutionary Studies in Imaginative Culture* 3, no. 1 (2019): 1–18. https://doi.org/10.26613/esic.3.1.110.

Menakem, Resmaa. *My Grandmother's Hands: Racialized Trauma and the Pathway to Mending Our Hearts and Bodies.* Central Recovery Press, 2017.

Rambo, Shelly. *Resurrecting Wounds: Living in the Afterlife of Trauma.* Baylor University Press, 2018.

Rambo, Shelly. *Spirit and Trauma: A Theology of Remaining.* Presbyterian Publishing Corporation, 2010.

Russell, Anna. "Why So Many People Are Going 'No Contact' with Their Parents." *New Yorker*, August 30, 2024. https://www.newyorker.com/culture/annals-of-inquiry/why-so-many-people-are-going-no-contact-with-their-parents.

Schuster, Tara. *Glow in the F*cking Dark: Simple Practices to Heal Your Soul, from Someone Who Learned the Hard Way.* Random House, 2023. Kindle.

Schwartz, Richard C. *No Bad Parts: Healing Trauma and Restoring Wholeness with the Internal Family Systems Model.* Sounds True, 2021.

Smith, Emily Esfahani. "The Two Kinds of Stories We Tell About Ourselves." *TED Ideas* (blog), January 12, 2017. https://ideas.ted.com/the-two-kinds-of-stories-we-tell-about-ourselves/.

Swinton, John. *Raging with Compassion: Pastoral Responses to the Problem of Evil.* Wm. B. Eerdmans, 2007.

Thurman, Howard. *Jesus and the Disinherited.* Beacon, 2022.

van der Kolk, Bessel A. *The Body Keeps the Score: Brain, Mind, and Body in the Healing of Trauma.* Penguin, 2014.

Walker, Pete. *Complex PTSD: From Surviving to Thriving.* Azure Coyote, 2013.

White Woman Whisperer. *The White Woman Whisperer.* Accessed January 30, 2025. https://www.whitewomanwhisperer.com/.

Zak. "Storytelling." https://greatergood.berkeley.edu/article/item/how_stories_change_brain.

www.ingramcontent.com/pod-product-compliance
Lightning Source LLC
Jackson TN
JSHW080843200825
89231JS00001B/1